Curiosities

of

Cambridgeshire

A County Guide
to the Unusual

by

Ian MacEachern

S.B. Publications

This book is dedicated to Marjory and Lyndsey

First published in 1991 by S.B. Publications
Unit 2, The Old Station Yard, Pipe Gate, Nr. Market Drayton
Shropshire TF9 4HY

British Library Cataloguing in Publication Data
MacEachern, Ian
    Curiosities of Cambridgeshire:
    A county guide to the unusual.
    1. Cambridgeshire (England). Travel
    I. Title
    914.26504859

    ISBN 1-870708-64-4

Typeset and printed by Delmar Press (Colour Printers) Ltd., Nantwich, Cheshire
Bound by Manchester Free Press, Jersey Street, Manchester M4 6FP

CONTENTS

CONTENTS

CONTENTS

ACKNOWLEDGEMENTS

The author is indebted to Steve Benz of S.B. Publications for his enthusiasm, support and guidance in the production of this collection of curiosities.

BIBLIOGRAPHY/FURTHER READING

Royal Commission of Historical Monuments. West Cambridgeshire (1958).

Royal Commission of Historical Monuments. North Cambridgeshire (1972).

Royal Commission of Historical Monuments. Huntingdonshire (1926).

CAMBRIDGESHIRE

'O' Denotes villages referenced

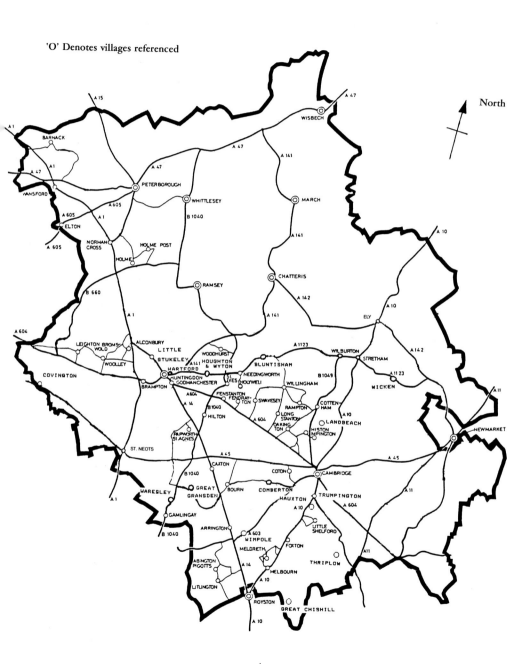

North

INTRODUCTION

Cambridgeshire has very few true follies: those costly ornamental structures of yesteryear. The Gothic Tower in the grounds of Wimpole Hall and the Moon Gate at Gamlingay Cinques are perhaps the only two such structures of any note, the latter badly overgrown and hardly noticeable by the casual passer by. However, Cambridgeshire does possess, although many people may not realise, a wealth of objects and structures from eras long since past, which I have called 'Cambridgeshire Curiosities'.

Progress is necessary and inevitably change follows on, invariably for the better. Today we turn a tap and water gushes forth, but not many years ago yokes and pails were used to fetch water from public pumps first introduced at the beginning of the 19th century to replace open wells. Many of these pumps still exist, although not necessarily in working order. Rampton's and Landbeach's 'double decker' pumps evoke scenes of an era when horse drawn bowsers drew alongside to be filled from the top spouts for crop irrigation or fire fighting purposes.

As one travels down Cambridgeshire's roads there is much of significance to be noticed; a lichen covered stone, upon closer inspection, can often turn out to be an old milestone or the remains of an ancient wayside cross. Look more carefully at what first appears to be an old shed or garage and you can discover an old bier house, fire engine house or village lock-up. A walk through a village churchyard, perusing old headstones, can reveal many fascinating epitaphs from the past.

Although flat the county is far from uninteresting; it is possible, for example, in just one short journey, to see bronze Age burial mounds, fields with ploughing marks left by Saxons, a watermill turned by a river that has worked a mill there since Domesday times and medieval stocks and whipping post.

In this book is a collection of photographs which I hope will stimulate the reader to look afresh at Cambridgeshire's countryside and what it has to offer. All of the objects and structures illustrated have played an important part, at some time or another, in shaping village life today, and I wish the reader much enjoyment in his or her discovery of further 'Cambridgeshire Curiosities'.

Ian J. O. MacEachern

THE ORIGIN OF BIG BEN'S CHIMES

> *Position:* The clock of Great St. Mary's Church, Cambridge.
> *Ordnance Map:* 1:50,000 Cambridge, Newmarket and surrounding area.
> *Sheet No:* Landranger 154
> *Map Reference:* 448585

Access: Exit the M11 at junction 13 on to the A1303 for Cambridge. Continue on the A1303 to the crossroads at the junction of Northampton Street, Chesterton Street, Castle Street and Magdalene Street. Turn right into Magdalene Street and follow the road into Bridge Street and then Sydney Street. Turn right into Market Street and follow to St. Mary's Street.

In 1793 the University erected a new clock in the west wall of the tower and a chime was composed by two undergraduates, one of whom was probably William Crotch who later became a distinguished composer of church music. They were said to have been inspired by Handel's aria 'I know that my Redeemer liveth'. It is now familiar to many millions beyond Cambridge since it was adopted first for the Royal Exchange in London and then for Big Ben. The sound of the Westminster chimes which were heard with hope by many in the dark days of the Second World War are then in reality Great St. Mary's or Cambridge chimes. Prior to the installation of a mechanical clock, the church's grand sundial, depicted above the west door, was used to tell the time.

There was a church on this site in the 11th century. It was rebuilt in 1298, and the existing church, sponsored by the University, dates from 1478. For centuries Great St. Mary's was used by the University for religious, academic and public functions. Like St. Mary's at Oxford, the church is not only a part of the main street but also of the forum academicum; it was used for examinations and degree ceremonies before the Schools were built in the 14th century. It was closely associated with the Reformation; Erasmus, Cranmer, Ridley and Latimer preached here. Martin Bucer was buried in the church in 1551, but his corpse was exhumed and publicly burnt outside in Mary's reign. It is said that Oliver Cromwell had the Book of Common Prayer destroyed here in his presence. Although still used for University services Great St. Mary's is also a parish church; the Mayor and Corporation have come here for civic services for many centuries.

BURIAL PLACE OF THE HEAD OF OLIVER CROMWELL

Position: Ante-chapel of Sydney Sussex College, Cambridge.
Ordnance Map: 1:50,000 Cambridge, Newmarket and surrounding area.
Sheet No: Landranger 154
Map Reference: 450587

Access: Exit the M11 at junction 13 on to the A1303 for Cambridge. Continue on the A1303 to the crossroads at the junction of Northampton Street, Chesterton Street, Castle Street and Magdalene Street. Turn right into Magdalene Street and follow the road into Bridge Street and then Sydney Street. Sydney Sussex College is on the left-hand side. The chapel is at the rear of the courtyard.

Following the Restoration, Cromwell was voted a traitor by Parliament and his body was exhumed in January 1661 and submitted to a traitor's execution. The head was cut off and placed on a pole at Westminster Hall for over 20 years. Oliver Cromwell was a Sydney Sussex man. In the College ante-chapel an oval plaque marks the grave, nearby, of his head, brought there in 1960 after a long residence with an Anglican canon in Suffolk. The plaque reads:

Near to this place was buried
on 25 March 1960 the head of
OLIVER CROMWELL
Lord Protector of the Commonwealth
of England, Scotland and Ireland,
Fellow Commoner of this College
1616-7

His body probably lies in the gallows pit at Tyburn.

HOBSON'S CONDUIT

Position: At the corner of Lensfield Road and Trumpington Street, Cambridge.

Ordnance Map: 1:50,000 Cambridge, Newmarket and surrounding area.

Sheet No: Landranger 154

Map Reference: 451577

Access: Exit the M11 at junction 12 on to the A603 for Cambridge. Follow the A603 along Barton Road, Newnham Road and the Fen Causeway to Trumpington Street. Turn left and then first right into Lensfield Road. Hobson's Conduit is at the junction of these 2 roads.

In 1614 a joint enterprise of the university and the town of Cambridge brought a supply of running water into the town from springs at Great Shelford. Thomas Hobson, the Carrier (1544-1630), was a benefactor of the scheme and for that reason the watercourse became known as 'Hobson's Conduit'.

This monument marks the end of the artificial watercourse. From this point the water runs in culverts to re-appear in runnels in Trumpington Street and St. Andrew's Street. Other culverts also feed ponds situated in the grounds of other colleges. From 1614-1856 the monument stood upon Market Hill where it served as a fountain. In the latter year, following the provision of a piped supply of water by the Cambridge Water Company, the "fountain" was moved to this site. It was reconditioned in 1967.

The plaque in front of the "fountain" was erected by the Hobson's Conduit Trustees and unveiled by the Mayor of Cambridge, Councillor M. N. Bradford, J.P. on 25 April 1967.

The inscribed stone on the "fountain" reads:

This Structure stood upon the Market Hill and served as a Conduit from 1614-1856 in which year it was re-erected on this spot by Public Subscription.

4

MOON/SUNDIAL

Position: Front Court, Queens College, Cambridge.
Ordnance Map: 1:50,000 Cambridge, Newmarket and surrounding area.
Sheet No: Landranger 154
Map Reference: 447582

Access: Exit the M11 at juction 13 on to the A1303 for Cambridge. Continue on the A1303 to the crossroads at the junction of Northampton Street, Chesterton Street, Castle Street and Magdalene Street. Turn right into Magdalene Street and follow the road into Bridge Street. Take first right into St. John's Street. Continue along to King's Parade then turn right into King's Lane and then Queen's Lane.

Above the south archway to the passage leading to the old Chapel is a single-light window similar to that east over the Ante-Chapel and these two flank a large painted sundial with the signs of the zodiac and tables of calculations below. The sundial is probably of mid-17th-century origin, but renewed in or shortly before 1733 and subsequently repainted. This magnificent sundial also tells the time at night so long as there is a moon. The dial also provides the date, sunrise and sunset times and the altitude of the sun.

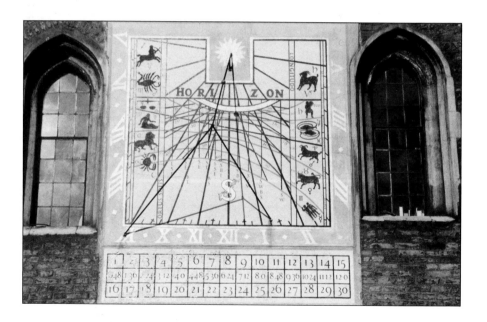

ST. JOHN'S COLLEGE ENTRANCE GATEWAY

Position: St. John's College, Cambridge.
Ordnance Map: 1:50,000 Cambridge, Newmarket and surrounding area.
Sheet No: Landranger 154
Map Reference: 448586

Access: Exit the M11 at junction 13 on to the A1303 for Cambridge. Continue on the A1303 to the crossroads at the junction of Northampton Street, Chesterton Street, Castle Street and Magdalene Street. Turn right into Magdalene Street and follow the road into Bridge Street. Take first right into St. John's Street.

The great front Gatehouse of St. John's College (1511-1516) has a splendidly decorated frontispiece which was repainted and restored in 1981. Like that at Christ's College, it pays tribute to the foundress, Henry VII's mother, Lady Margaret Beaufort, Countess of Richmond and Derby, whose coat of arms is displayed. The arms display strange looking animals known as yales, characterized by their goats' heads, antelopes' bodies and elephants' tails. The ground behind the yales is powdered with daisies and borage. Above the arms is a statue of the evangelist St. John; the work of George Woodroff in 1662.

THE 'ANONYMOUS' BOX

Position: Junction of Priory Road and Riverside, Cambridge.

Ordnance Map: 1:50,000 Cambridge, Newmarket and surrounding area.

Sheet No: Landranger 154

Map Reference: 462591

Access: Exit the M11 at juction 13 on to the A1303 for Cambridge. Continue on the A1303 to the roundabout at the junction with Elizabeth Way and turn right. After crossing the river turn left at the roundabout into Newmarket Road. Take the second left into River Lane. At the top of the road turn left into Riverside and continue to the junction with Priory Road.

The cylindrical-shaped post box was introduced in 1879, however, rather belatedly, it was not realised until 1887 that these boxes bore neither Royal cipher nor indication that the boxes were the property of the post office. This oversight was rectified by an alteration to the basic design. Some 300 of these so called 'anonymous' boxes are still in use; 5 of which are in Cambridge. The box at Priory Road is of most interest because of its spiked top.

THE PENFOLD BOX

Position: At the gateway to King's College, Cambridge.

Ordnance Map: 1:50,000 Cambridge, Newmarket and surrounding area.

Sheet No: Landranger 154

Map Reference: 447585

Access: Exit the M11 at junction 13 on to the A1303 for Cambridge. Continue on the A1303 to the crossroads at the junction of Northampton Street, Chesterton Street, Castle Street and Magdalene Street. Turn right into Magdalene Street and follow the road into Bridge Street. Take first right into St. John's Street and continue along to King's Parade.

In 1866 the post office introduced the first of the hexagonal post boxes known as the Penfold box, named after its designer J. W. Penfold. Some 56 of these boxes are still in use. Possibly, the most used Penfold box, which is also the only one in the county, is the one which stands outside the gateway into King's College — No. 104 King's College Post Box.

THE ROUND CHURCH

Position: Off Bridge Street, Cambridge.
Ordnance Map: 1:50,000 Cambridge, Newmarket and surrounding area.
Sheet No: Landranger 154 ·
Map Reference: 448588

Access: Exit the M11 at juction 13 on to the A1303 for Cambridge. Continue on the A1303 to the crossroads at the junction of Northampton Street, Chesterton Street, Castle Street and Magdalene Street. Turn right into Magdalene Street and follow the road into Bridge Street. The church is on the left-hand side at the junction with Round Church Street.

The Round Church, constructed circa 1130 midway between the first two Crusades, was modelled on the plan of the Holy Sepulchre in Jerusalem and replaced a still earlier church of St. George. It was rebuilt by Salvin in 1842. The stubby columns and circular ground plan are original, but the round clerestory and cone are replacements for the original 16-sided belltower. It is one of four round churches still in use in England; the other three being the church of the Holy Sepulchre at Northampton, the temple Church in London which was erected by the Knights Templars and the Baptist Church at Little Maplestead in Essex which used to belong to the Knights Hospitallers.

A TRINITY MILESTONE

Position: Near to the junction of Trumpington Road and Chaucer Road, Cambridge.
Ordnance Map: 1:50,000 Cambridge, Newmarket and surrounding area.
Sheet No: Landranger 154
Map Reference: 452569

Access: Take the A1134 from Cambridge for Trumpington. The Mile Post is situated on the right-hand side of Trumpington Road, next to the traffic light controlled junction to Brooklands Avenue, on the left, and Chaucer Road, on the right.

This milestone is one of a number of 'Trinity Milestones' erected along the old Cambridge to London road via Fowlmere and Barkway; said to be the very first milestones in England. The distances were measured from a datum point marked by a circular disc cut in 1732 on the outside south-west buttress of the tower of Great St. Mary's Church, in Cambridge, some 2 or 3 feet above ground level; Robert Hare of Caius College left the money for their erection. They bear a crescent and rings within an ornamental shield, the arms of Trinity College, for it was the Master of that College, Dr. Warren, who did the work.

COMBERTON WATER PUMP

Position: Comberton, 5 miles west of Cambridge.
Ordnance Map: 1:50,000 Cambridge, Newmarket and surrounding area.
Sheet No: Landranger 154
Map Reference: 382563

Access: Take the A603 from Cambridge for Barton. After crossing over the M11, turn right on to the B1046 for Comberton. The pump is on the village green.

Cast-iron hand water pump as used by bucket-carrying villagers with a yoke across their shoulders to balance two buckets.

MONUMENT TO ANDREW DOWNES

Position: Inside St. Peter's Church, Coton, 2 miles west of Cambridge.

Ordnance Map: 1:50,000 Cambridge, Newmarket and surrounding area.

Sheet No: Landranger 154

Map Reference: 408589

Access: Take A1303 west from Cambridge. After 2 miles exit left on to the minor road for Coton village. The monument is inside the 12th century Church of St. Peter set into the wall to the right of the altar.

Andrew Downes was one of the Cambridge group of translators who produced the Authorised Version of the Bible. His group had special responsibility for the Apocrypha, but Downes was also one of the six scholars who gave the whole work final revision before its publication.

The painted wall memorial was restored in 1968 through the generosity of the Master and Fellows of St. John's College, Cambridge.

The Downes Memorial bears a Latin inscription, whose translation is as follows:

Andrew Downes came from Shropshire. He was a Fellow of St. John's College, Cambridgeshire and Regius Professor of Greek. His service in this post lasted 39 years. It was most faithful and brought distinction to his Chair and exceptional praise to himself.

He was a man of shining sincerity of character. In Divinity his work was thorough and sound, and in the whole range of civilized learning, his very quiet understanding and experience were astonishing. When he was well over 70, the University relieved him of his duties but nevertheless, as a mark of respect to him, continued his usual emoluments.

In the 77th year of his age, he withdrew from the town to his country place close by, and here it was that before a year had passed, he laid aside his mortal state on the 2nd February 1627.

TABLE OF THE DECALOGUE

Position: In the ground stage of tower of St. Peter's Church, Coton, 2 miles west of Cambridge.

Ordnance Map: 1:50,000 Cambridge, Newmarket and surrounding area.

Sheet No: Landranger 154

Map Reference: 408589

Access: Take A1303 west from Cambridge. After 2 miles exit left on to the minor road for Coton village.

The Table of the Decalogue (the Ten Commandments) is written on a framed board, under the tower, with moulded cornice and pediment painted with the emblem of the Deity and clouds. The 18th-century text has flaked off in parts revealing similar black-letter inscriptions of the late 16th and 17th century.

VILLAGE PUMP — COTON

Position: On the small village green east of St. Peter's Church, Coton, 2 miles
    west of Cambridge.
Ordnance Map: 1:50,000 Cambridge, Newmarket and surrounding area.
Sheet No: Landranger 154
Map Reference: 409589

Access: Take A1303 west from Cambridge. After 2 miles exit left on to the minor
road for Coton village.

Coton settlement is on a spring-line, the position of the main water supply, which
was perhaps the 'petrifying spring' described by Gardner, being preserved in the
name 'Well Close', the site of a moat within which now stands the Rectory. The
public supply was located on the small green where the village pump still stands at
the north-west corner of the Rectory moat and immediately east of the church. A
second pump can be found in front of the church.

A FINE CHURCH SUNDIAL — COTTENHAM

Position: On side of All Saints Church tower, Cottenham.
Ordnance Map: 1:50,000 Cambridge, Newmarket and surrounding area.
Sheet No: Landranger 154.
Map Reference: 455686.

Access: Take B1049 from Cambridge for Histon and Cottenham.

Most churches had a sundial until it was made redundant by a mechanical clock. Nowadays one must travel many miles to see one. Cottenham church, built in the Perpendicular style of the 15th century with pineapple pinnacles on the tower, has a particularly fine example of a sundial, bearing the legend 'The Time is Short'.

RECORD OF THE FALL OF COTTENHAM CHURCH SPIRE

> *Position:* Slate tablet on the inside wall of the All Saint's church porch, Cottenham, 6 miles north of Cambridge.
> *Ordnance Map:* 1:50,000 Cambridge, Newmarket and surrounding area.
> *Sheet No:* Landranger 154.
> *Map Reference:* 455686.

Access: Take the B1049 from Cambridge for Histon and then Cottenham. The church is at the end of the very long main street, which starts at Green End in the south and finishes at Church End in the north.

Set among chestnuts and yews in Church Close, All Saints' great attraction is the spectacular design of its Jacobean tower, which stands on a base of silvery ashlar rising through white gault brick to a bright red brick and a stepped stone parapet with 4 stone corner pinnacles, bulbous like small Orthodox domes, which make it one of Cambridgeshire's landmarks. Donors' names, carved in 1617, adorn the tower. 1617 was the year the tower lost its spire. A slate tablet inside the front porch, which was originally in the school house which stood close by the church states:

This School-house being demolished by the Fall of the Steeple A.D. 1617 was rebuilt A.D. 1699 at the Charge of Mrs. Kathrin Pepys who also Gave a Commonable House And 100 in money for the Teaching of Poor Children. Also She Gave to ye Town of Rance 100 in money for ye use of ye Poor.

SCRATCH-DIAL, HAUXTON CHURCH

> *Position:* The sun dial is to the right of the entrance to St. Edmund's Church, Hauxton, near Cambridge.
>
> *Ordnance Map:* 1:50,000 Cambridge, Newmarket and surrounding area.
>
> *Sheet No:* Landranger 154.
>
> *Map Reference:* 436522.

Access: Take A1309 from Cambridge for Royston. At the roundabout, junction 11 of the M11, take the A10(T) for Harston. After one mile turn left on to the minor road for Hauxton. St. Edmund's Church is on the left-hand side as one enters Hauxton.

Hard building stone had to be imported into the Cambridgeshire region. Thus 'clunch', the local soft chalk, was the main building material for most of the early domestic buildings, and expensive imported stone was, therefore, reserved for the wall corners, windows and door-posts. Consequently, many of the village churches were built of brown pebble and flints from the chalky subsoil. Bigger and harder stones were also incorporated and often put to good use, as with this stone in the wall of Hauxton Church, upon which there is a scratch sun-dial.

HISTON'S BOXED VILLAGE PUMP

Position: Next to the village green in Histon, 4 miles north-west of Cambridge.
Ordnance Map: 1:50,000 Cambridge, Newmarket and surrounding area.
Sheet No: Landranger 154.
Map Reference: 440636.

Access: Take the B1049 from Cambridge for Histon. Turn left at the traffic light junction for Girton and Oakington on to the minor road, The Green. The pump is on the right next to the village pond.

Histon's village green is exceptionally pretty; a brook runs through it on which can be found many ducks, and it is surrounded by many old and historic houses. There used to be two large barns behind the house, pictured left in the background, which were destroyed by fire. In 1858 they were used for a public tea and an evening meeting on the occasion of the laying of the foundation stone for the original Baptist Chapel. C. H. Spurgeon preached two sermons, to large congregations, in one of these barns. The mounted village pump, which is boxed, still stands in its original position. It is thought that at one time stocks stood nearby. The pump was restored in 1984 by the Histon & Impington Village Society in memory of Ken Oates, a local historian, who died in 1981 at the age of 76 years.

MOSES CARTER'S STONE

Position: In the car park of The Boot public house, Histon 4 miles north-west
of Cambridge.
Ordnance Map: 1:50,000 Cambridge, Newmarket and surrounding area.
Sheet No: Landranger 154.
Map Reference: 438636.

Access: Take the B1049 from Cambridge for Histon. The Boot public house is at the junction of High Street and Station Road, opposite the Post Office. The stone lies in a flower bed at the end of the car park off High Street.

Moses Carter, the genial Histon Giant, was over seven feet tall. He carried the great boulder from the Ballast Hole in Park Lane to The Boot public house for a bet. As no one else could lift the stone, it still lies there today. Moses loved children, and apparently lived on boiled beef and dumplings. He was born early last century, died in the 1860s, and is buried in Histon churchyard. His tall hat and one of his boots are still in existence. Moses is remembered in the wrought iron village sign, which stands opposite the village green near to the Boot Inn.

'DOUBLE-DECKER' PUMP

Position: On the small green at the junction of High Street and Spaldings Lane in Landbeach near Cambridge.
Ordnance Map: 1:50,000 Cambridge, Newmarket and surrounding area.
Sheet No: Landranger 154.
Map Reference: 476654.

Access: Take the A10(T) from Cambridge to Ely. After crossing over the A45(T) road, north of Cambridge, exit left on to the minor road for Landbeach.

Water is one of the essentials and is vital to life. In the past springs and streams used to provide most villages with a ready supply of water, which were often supplemented by open wells, with a bucket and winding-gear on top. However, during the 19th century, many of these open wells were replaced with a cast-iron water pump from which, morning and evening, the villagers would collect their water in galvanised pails. These communal pumps were used well into this century, for example, Whittlesford's was in use up until 1966. Landbeach's pump is a fine example of a 'double-decker'. The top-spout was used for filling water carts. It is also boxed, that is encased in wood, as a protection against frost.

20

REMAINS OF MEDIEVAL ABBEY

Position: 3 miles north of Landbeach off A10(T) road.
Ordnance Map: 1:50,000 Cambridge, Newmarket and surrounding area.
Sheet No: Landranger 154.
Map Reference: 492685.

Access: Approximately 8 miles south of Ely on A10(T) road. Denny Abbey signposted on left after passing through Chittering.

Denny Abbey is a Medieval Abbey which was later converted to a farmhouse. Building started about 1159 and it became a religious house for 3 different monastic orders. From 1159 it was a monastery for a small community of Benedictine monks, an off-shoot of Ely Abbey which is now the cathedral.

In 1170 it became a home for aged and infirm Knights Templars — an Order of soldier-monks formed during the crusades against the Moslems in the Holy Land.

From 1342 it housed nuns of the Franciscan Order of Minoresses (the Sisters of Poor Clare). It also incorporated private apartments for the foundress Mary, Countess of Pembroke, who had moved the nuns from nearby Waterbeach.

After the Dissolution of the monasteries by Henry VIII in 1536, Denny Abbey became a farm house, and was occupied as such up until the Second World War.

It is now looked after by English Heritage. The building, from this angle, looks most like a church. One can see the north transept on the left and, adjoining it, the 2-bay nave of the original Benedictine Monk's church. Note the richly decorated west door of the Templar's church and the outline of the west window filled in with brick. Until recently this was hidden by later buildings. The addition on the right side dates from the 13th century. It may well have been built to house a priest when Denny was in use as a hospital for the Knights Templars' Order. To the left was the nuns' cloister and their dormitory leading out from the north transept. A rectangular grille covers the water cistern used throughout the monastic period.

LANDBEACH PARISH POUND

Position: Opposite the small green at the junction of High Street and Spaldings Lane in Landbeach near Cambridge.

Ordnance Map: 1:50,000 Cambridge, Newmarket and surrounding area.

Sheet No: Landranger 154.

Map Reference: 476655.

Access: Take A10(T) from Cambridge to Ely. After crossing over the A45(T) road, north of Cambridge, exit left on to the minor road for Landbeach.

Village Pounds were used to impound cattle that had strayed from common grazing.

LONGSTANTON WATER PUMP

Position: At the entrance to Striplands Farm, on the northern outskirts of Longstanton village, 7 miles north-west of Cambridge.

Ordnance Map: 1:50,000 Cambridge, Newmarket and surrounding area.

Sheet No: Landranger 154.

Map Reference: 395674.

Access: Take A604(T) from Cambridge to Huntingdon. Exit on to the B1050 road for Longstanton. Drive through the village towards Willingham.

The pump is a fine example of a Bamford's Frost Protected Lift Pump.

BAPTISMAL WELL

Position: Inside the churchyard of St. Michael's Church, Longstanton 7 miles
north-west of Cambridge.
Ordnance Map: 1:50,000 Cambridge, Newmarket and surrounding area.
Sheet No: Landranger 154.
Map Reference: 398664.

Access: Take A604(T) from Cambridge towards Huntingdon. Exit on to the B1050
for Longstanton. St. Michael's Church is at the south-eastern end of the village.

The ancient church of St. Michael's, one of only two thatched churches in
Cambridgeshire, stands in a neat churchyard with a large chestnut tree just inside its
gate. Under the tree there is a canopied well with steps leading down to the water.
The well was a holy baptism well and is thought to be very old. It was restored and
its railings replaced by the villagers in 1986. The church, although no longer required
for regular worship, remains consecrated to the Service of God. It is maintained by
the Redundant Churches Fund, St. Andrew-by-the-Wardrobe, Queen Victoria Street,
London EC4V 5DE with monies provided by Parliament, by the Church of England
and by the gifts of the public.

A reminder of Longstanton's long gone windmills can be found at St. Michael's
where a set of old millstones have been used as a paved entrance to the churchyard.

TOMB OF THE 3 NON-CONFORMIST MARTYRS

Position: In a small garden just outside the wall of the parish church of
St. Andrew, Oakington.
Ordnance Map: 1:50,000 Cambridge, Newmarket and surrounding area.
Sheet No: Landranger 154.
Map Reference: 415648.

Access: Take A604(T) leading north-west from Cambridge towards Huntingdon.
After approximately one mile, exit for Oakington on minor road.

Oakington lies in the heart of Cromwell country and throughout the 17th century
was a stronghold of religious independence. The most famous of the dissenters was
the Congregationalist Francis Holcroft, known as 'the Apostle of East Anglia'. He
was buried in 1692 just outside Oakington churchyard by the side of his assistant
Joseph Oddey and Henry Osland, the pastor of the first Congregationalist church in
the area. For many years visitors to the 'Oakington Graves' have assumed that the
dissenters had been denied burial in sanctified ground, but recent research has shown
that the non-conformists had bought a field adjoining the churchyard as a cemetery
of their own. Inscriptions read as follows:

Here Lyeth the Body
of Mr. Henry Oseland
Minister of the Gospel
who after 17 yrs faithful
Dispensation of the same in
ye Church gathered at
Willington and Cottenham
ended this life 19 Nov 1711
aged 43 yrs.

Here lyeth buryed the
body of Mr. Joseph Oddey
Minister of the Gospel, deceased
the 3rd May 1687. Mark the
perfect man, and behold the
upright for the end of that
man is peace.

Here lieth the body of
Mr. Francis Holcroft, Minister
of the Gospel who died
Jan 6th 1692 aged 59 yrs.

Daniel 12th V:3

And they that be wise shall shine as
the brightness of the firmament; and
they that turn many be righteousness
as the stars for ever and ever.

TO THE GLORY OF GOD

FRANCIS HOLCROFT
(1633 ~ 1692)
'The Apostle of Cambridgeshire'
AND
JOSEPH ODDY
(1629 ~ 1687)

17th Century Pioneers of Nonconformity
in this Area.

RAMPTON'S 'DOUBLE-DECKER' PUMP

> *Position:* On the Green at Rampton, 6 miles north of Cambridge.
> *Ordnance Map:* 1:50,000 Cambridge, Newmarket and surrounding area.
> *Sheet No:* Landranger 154.
> *Map Reference:* 426679.

Access: Take the B1049 from Cambridge for Histon and then Cottenham. At Cottenham take the left-hand junction, by the village green, for Rampton.

Rampton's white-painted boxed 'double-decker' pump, similar to the one at Landbeach, stands beneath a fine plane tree. Near to the pump, on this small but attractive triangular green, is the foot of an old prayer cross underneath which modern artifacts have been buried in a time capsule for future generations. The green is also planted with chestnut trees and is the site of the annual village Feast Fair. It is believed that in medieval times salt must have been sold at some of the Fair stalls, as many early attempts, by the Parish Council, at planting further trees failed due to high soil salinity.

14th-CENTURY FIGURE OF DE L'ISLE

> *Position:* Inside the chancel of All Saints Church, Rampton, 6 miles north of Cambridge.
> *Ordnance Map:* 1:50,000 Cambridge, Newmarket and surrounding area.
> *Sheet No:* Landranger 154.
> *Map Reference:* 428681.

Access: Take the B1049 from Cambridge for Histon and then Cottenham. At Cottenham take the left-hand junction, by the village green, for Rampton. The church is on the right-hand side of the road at the entrance to the village and opposite The Old School Building.

The Church of All Saints is unusual in that its roof is half thatched. This is because when the Norman chancel was replaced, in the 14th century, it was not re-thatched. The chancel floor is paved with old pamments and several fragments of late Anglo-Saxon stone coffin lids can be found in the east wall. The rather eroded stone figure of de L'Isle lies grasping his sword with his shield on his shoulder. He was probably the builder of the chancel. Also of note is the well preserved Elizabethan pulpit complete with tester, and the double piscina.

To the right of the red brick 18th-century porch, on the exterior of the south wall near to the roof eaves, there is a stone inscribed with the words 'In Hoc Signo Vinces AD 1910' and lettered C, H, E and W in its 4 corners. Also of note, low down on the south chancel wall, is a small iron grated opening, now boarded up, similar to the one at Bluntisham's church, which was used for ringing the Sanctus Bell.

Finally, set into the east wall below the chancel window, there is a tablet inscribed as follows:

AD 1924 To the Glory of God This window is erected in memory of HUGH GERARD EVELYN-WHITE MA here interred who actively promoted the work: the REV THOMAS GURNEY, JOHANNA C. GURNEY, and the men of this Village who fell in the Great War. Jesu Mercy.

GIANT'S HILL

Position: In a field close to the Church of All Saints in Rampton, 6 miles north of Cambridge.

Ordnance Map: 1:50,000 Cambridge, Newmarket and surrounding area.

Sheet No: Landranger 154.

Map Reference: 431681.

Access: Take the B1049 from Cambridge for Histon and then Cottenham. At Cottenham take the left-hand junction, by the village green, for Rampton. The Giant's Hill is signposted at a lay-by on the right-hand side of the road at the entrance to Rampton.

Giant's Hill, willow screened and set in a cow pasture, is an ancient earthwork dating back to the time of King Stephen, which appears to be another of the forts ordered by Stephen which, like Burwell Castle, became redundant when Mandeville was killed by an arrow in 1144. The Hill, its moat and the ripples from ridge and furrow ploughing are all that now remain. Another old inconspicuous oval earthwork, only 880 feet at its broadest, Belsar's Hill, lies near to Rampton on the single-track road, via The Irams, to Willingham. It lies athwart the main medieval approach from Cambridge to Aldreth Causway and Ely. It is possibly the remains of an Iron Age fort, but it was almost certainly used in William the Conqueror's attack on Hereward as in 1221 its name was Bellasise, Norman-French for 'lovely seat'.

THE OLD SCHOOL

Position: Opposite the Church of All Saints in Rampton, 6 miles north
of Cambridge.
Ordnance Map: 1:50,000 Cambridge, Newmarket and surrounding area.
Sheet No: Landranger 154.
Map Reference: 428679.

Access: Take the B1049 from Cambridge for Histon and then Cottenham. At
Cottenham take the left-hand junction, by the village green, for Rampton. The Old
School is on the left-hand side of the road at the entrance to the village and
opposite the Church of All Saints.

The Old School is now a private house. Of note is the open bell tower; the bell is
missing.

THE WALE OBELISK

Position: Approximately 1 mile south-east of Little Shelford, near Cambridge.
Ordnance Map: 1:50,000 Cambridge, Newmarket and surrounding area.
Sheet No: Landranger 154.
Map Reference: 442507.

Access: Take A1309 from Cambridge for Royston. At the roundabout, junction 11 of the M11, take the A10(T) for Harston. On entering Harston, turn left onto the B1368 for Newton. Approximately 3/4 miles further on turn left for Little Shelford (signposted the Shelfords). About 500 yards down this road, on the right-hand side, is a small lay-by and public footpath sign-posted to the obelisk.

The slender obelisk is at the top of a small hill, Maggots (short for Margaret's) Mount, which affords panoramic views of the surrounding countryside. The stone pillar, which is over 250 years old, is mounted on a concrete pyramidal plinth and holds a flame of liberty aloft. It was restored by public subscription in 1985 by Rattee & Kett Ltd, stonemasons. The obelisk is signed by Charles Bottomley, circa 1739, and commemorates Gregory Wale. The inscription on it reads:

> *To the memory of Gregory Wale Esq*
> *Justice of the Peace for this County,*
> *Deputy Lieutenant, County Treasurer,*
> *Conservator of the River Cam.*
> *He lived an advocate for Liberty.*
> *A good subject, an agreeable companion,*
> *A faithful friend, an hospitable neighbour*
> *And in all parts of life a useful member of society.*
> *He died June 5th 1739, in the 71st year of his age.*
> *Universally lamented and was buried in the Parish of*
> *Little Shelford. This obelisk was erected by his*
> *surviving friend JAMES CHURCH Esq as a public testimony*
> *of his regard to the memory of so worthy a gentleman.*

OLD GRANARY — TRINITY COLLEGE FARM

Position: At Trinity College farm, which is now derelict, near Swavesey,
8 miles west of Cambridge.
Ordnance Map: 1:50,000 Cambridge, Newmarket and surrounding area.
Sheet No: Landranger 154.
Map Reference: 375667.

Access: Take A604(T) from Cambridge for Huntingdon. Exit on to the minor road
for Swavesey. After approximately one and a half miles turn right on to the minor
road for Longstanton. After a further mile turn right on to a farm road for
Highfield Farm. The derelict farm buildings of Trinity College Farm are on the left-
hand side and ½ mile down this track.

Small grain stores mounted on either brick piers or mushroom-shaped stones, known
as saddle or staddle stones, used to be a common sight. Most date from the early
18th century. The buildings were timber clad with a peg-tile pyramidal roof and
often incorporated with dovecotes.

WILLINGHAM PUMP

Position: On the village green at Willingham, 9 miles north-west of Cambridge.
Ordnance Map: 1:50,000 Cambridge, Newmarket and surrounding area.
Sheet No: Landranger 154.
Map Reference: 408704.

Access: Take A604(T) from Cambridge for Huntingdon. Exit on to the B1050 road for Longstanton and then Willingham.

Willingham's pump is sited on a brick plinth and encased in wood as a protection against frost. It is fitted with a splashguard and painted green similar to that of Longstanton's. It stands in the middle of the village green, which at one time had a village pond. The pump was used by farmers up until the 1950s. They would draw alongside and fill their water bowsers for crop irrigation. Similarly in earlier days the hand- and horse-drawn fire engine bowsers were filled from this pump.

ROOF ANGELS —
ST. MARY AND ALL SAINTS CHURCH

> *Position:* Roof of St. Mary and All Saints Church, Willingham, 9 miles
> north-west of Cambridge.
> *Ordnance Map:* 1:50,000 Cambridge, Newmarket and surrounding area.
> *Sheet No:* Landranger 154.
> *Map Reference:* 405705.

Access: Take A604(T) from Cambridge for Huntingdon. Exit on to the B1050 road
for Longstanton and then Willingham.

The roof has a double hammer-beam design in oak, thought to have been made in
the 15th century originally. Thus, it was already over 200 years old when it was
fitted at Willingham in 1613 as a second-hand roof, which is well illustrated by the
way in which the roof wall posts intrude over some of the clerestory windows and
the wall paintings. The roof is believed to have come from the ruined Barnwell
Priory in Cambridge, and without its complement of angels. The magnificent 36
angels currently adorning the roof, carrying emblems, musical instruments and
symbols of the Passion, were made and fitted in the 19th and 20th centuries.

SUNDIAL — ST. MARY AND ALL SAINTS CHURCH

Position: To the right of the south porch on the outside south wall of St. Mary and All Saints Church, Willingham, 9 miles north-west of Cambridge.
Ordnance Map: 1:50,000 Cambridge, Newmarket and surrounding area.
Sheet No: Landranger 154.
Map Reference: 405705.

Access: Take A604(T) from Cambridge for Huntingdon. Exit on to the B1050 road for Longstanton and then Willington.

Most churches had a sundial until they were superseded by mechanical clocks. The church at Willingham has both. The clock is by W. Potts & Sons of Leeds. It was made and fitted to the tower in 1887 following a public subscription. It is still wound twice weekly.

WILLINGHAM MILL

Position: At the bottom of Mill Lane, Willingham, 9 miles north-west of
Cambridge.
Ordnance Map: 1:50,000 Cambridge, Newmarket and surrounding area.
Sheet No: Landranger 154.
Map Reference: 404697.

Access: Take A604(T) from Cambridge for Huntingdon. Exit on to the B1050
road for Longstanton and then onto Willingham. At the crossroads in
Willingham turn right for Rampton, then take the next right-hand turn into
Mill Lane for the mill.

The mill was built by Mr. W. Huckle in 1828. It has been owned by the
Cattell family since 1875. A 100 years later it lay in a state of decay, having
ceased flour production in 1962. The mill is currently being restored by Mr.
Wallis Barton, whose father-in-law owns the mill, and Mr. Graham Wilson, a
millwright, who used to work at the mill when it was owned by C. Cattell &
Son. Mr. Wilson was one of the last wheelwrights to be trained. He bought
and restored Over windmill some 30 years ago. The restoration work, which
commenced in 1979, is being done by hand in the same fashion that it would
have been done when it was first built. The eventual aim is to restore the mill
to its full former glory, grinding corn and producing flour, and to be self-
sufficient financially through the sale of flour to healthfood manufacturers and
by opening the mill to the public. The restorers also hope to use the windmill's
power to create electricity for use within the mill. Inside the mill its large gear
mechanism is stamped with the initials W. R. and the date 1858.

The restoration work is being grant aided by South Cambridgeshire District
Council through its Historic Building Repair scheme. The mill cap was refitted
in 1989 and it is hoped to have the 4 sails back on by 1991.

13th-CENTURY WALL PAINTING OF ST. ETHELREDA

Position: Right-hand splay of the narrow lancet window in the west wall of St. Mary and All Saints Church, Willingham, 9 miles north-west of Cambridge.
Ordnance Map: 1:50,000 Cambridge, Newmarket and surrounding area.
Sheet No: Landranger 154.
Map Reference: 405705.

Access: Take A604(T) from Cambridge for Huntingdon. Exit on to the B1050 road for Longstanton and then Willingham.

This wall painting is the oldest known wall painting of St. Ethelreda, the foundress of the Monastery at Ely in 672. It was painted in the mid-13th century, possibly in honour of Henry III's visit in 1244, and can be identified as St. Ethelreda by the fresh wound in her neck, the result of the removal of a tumour during her last illness, which was recorded by Bede. The wound is known to feature on other medieval paintings of her. The painting was restored in 1979.

14th-CENTURY WALL PAINTING OF ST. CHRISTOPHER

Position: North wall of the nave of St. Mary and All Saints Church, Willingham, 9 miles north-west of Cambridge.
Ordnance Map: 1:50,000 Cambridge, Newmarket and surrounding area.
Sheet No: Landranger 154.
Map Reference: 405705.

Access: Take A604(T) from Cambridge for Huntingdon. Exit on to the B1050 road for Longstanton and then Willingham.

This wall painting was done about 1380. It was restored in 1983 and is now considered to be the finest complete wall painting of St. Christopher in the country. Christopher's head was covered by one of the roof wall posts from the fitting of the 'new' roof in 1613 right up until 1983; hence the richness of colour there. Of note is the range of marine life in the water around his feet: a whale or porpoise, a serpent and various common fish. Also of note are the six fingers of St. Christopher's left hand, and the beautifully portrayed sensitivity in the face of the Christchild held in his arm.

40

BOURN MILL

Position: On rising ground at the east edge of the parish near the outskirts
of Caxton, 10 miles south-east of Huntingdon.
Ordnance Map: 1:50,000 Bedford, Huntingdon and surrounding area.
Sheet No: Landranger 153.
Map Reference: 312580.

Access: Take the A1198, formerly the A14, from Huntingdon for Royston. At Caxton
turn left on to the minor road for Bourn. The mill is on the left-hand side of
the road.

The windmill is of the post
type, framed and boarded, with
a pitched roof of overlapping
boards, and was built in the
first half of the 17th century or
earlier. It was later enlarged by
enclosing the rear platform.
Repaired in 1874. Presented to
the Cambridge Preservation
Society in 1932 and was once
again repaired and reinforced in
collaboration with the Office of
Works in the succeeding year.
It is one of the best preserved
in Britain. The machinery is in
general 19th century. An
inscription "E BISMUR 1758"
on a first floor stud probably
records a repair.

CAXTON GIBBET

Position: One and a half miles north of Caxton, at roundabout, intersection of A45(T) and A14, Royston to Huntingdon road.
Ordnance Map: 1:50,000 Bedford, Huntingdon and surrounding area.
Sheet No: Landranger 153.
Map Reference: 296606.

Access: Take A14 from Godmanchester for Royston. After passing through Papworth Everard, arrive, one and a half miles further on, at A45(T) and A14 roundabout. The gibbet is in the corner of the car park of the Caxton Gibbet Inn, which is on the east side of the A14 across from the roundabout.

Caxton's one-armed raddled wooden gibbet, which is a replica, is the sole remaining gibbet in the county. It stands atop a little mound within the grounds of the inn named after it, the Caxton Gibbet Inn. It was last used for the son of a former landlord of this Inn. He murdered three of the guests and hid their bodies in a well under the stairs.

Caxton gibbet is associated with many tales and stories. It is said that a murderer was once hung there in an iron cage and left to starve to death, but that a baker took pity on him and gave him some bread whereupon he was promptly hung up with the felon. Another tale is that it was erected in 1753 to hang a Royston highwayman called Gatwood, who had been holding up stagecoaches on the Great North Road. During the second world war it was used to hang effigies of Hitler and his henchmen.

42

GAMLINGAY ALMSHOUSES

Position: Numbers 42-60 Church Street, Gamlingay, 6 miles north-east
of Biggleswade.
Ordnance Map: 1:50,000 Bedford, Huntingdon and surrounding area.
Sheet No: Landranger 153.
Map Reference: 239523.

Access: Take the A1198, formerly the A14, from Huntingdon for Royston. Turn left
for Longstowe and the Gransdens at the crossroads with the B1046, 3½ miles on
from the Caxton Gibbet roundabout. Then turn sharp left onto the minor road for
Gamlingay after a further 3½ miles.

In 1600, the sins of Gamlingay's forefathers were purged in fire and flame. Nobody
knows how the blaze started, although some say it was the work of a wandering
vagabond with a grudge against the villagers for "their meanness and uncharity".
Whether true or not Gamlingay was devastated. Only the church remained
unscathed. Sixty five years later John Bunyan came to the village. His exhortations
were delivered in a barn for it was not until 1710 that the Baptist Chapel was built.
Bunyan may or may not have stirred up the village conscience but in 1665, the
Plague Year, Sir John Jacob constructed a block of almshouses in what is now
Church Street. The will of William Mainstone, who died in 1683, included a bequest
for the repair of the almshouses, and nearly a 100 years after their construction, they
were endowed by Mrs. Elizabeth Lane for the benefit of eight poor ladies out of the
proceeds of certain South Sea Island annuities.

The almshouses consist of 10 tenements forming an east and west terrace on the
south side of Church Street; a chapel was added at the east end in 1745. They are
two-storeyed, of brick, with continuous tiled roof. Each tenement consists of a single
room on either floor. Behind are enclosed yards. The street elevation is
symmetrically designed about the tablet, which is framed in scrollwork with a broken
pediment enclosing a shield of arms of Jacob and the inscription:

> *VIVAT obi NATUS*
> *Johannes Jacob*
> *Miles & Baro'ius*
> *Anno Domini 1665*

Either side of the tablet are moulded brick frames each divided into four arcs by
projecting keystones. The two-panelled entrance doors, with fanlights above, are
flanked by large wooden windows with flat arches each divided into six lights by
mullions and a transom with iron casements.

44

THE MOON GATE

Position: In a field off the minor road from Gamlingay Cinques to Everton, north-east of Sandy, Bedfordshire.
Ordnance Map: 1:50,000 Bedford, Huntingdon and surrounding area.
Sheet No: Landranger 153.
Map Reference: 223527.

Access: Take the A1198, formerly the A14, from Huntingdon to Royston. At the outskirts of Papworth Everard turn left on to the B1040 for Eltisley. At the junction with the A45(T) turn right then next left back onto the B1040 for Waresley and then Gamlingay. At Gamlingay turn right onto Cinques Road. Proceed on this road upto the crossroads and then turn left for Everton and Sandy. A short distance down this road, on the left, is the Moon Gate in a field, shrouded by trees. Access is by Public Footpath, which is signposted.

The Full Moon Gate, built of red brick in 1712 by Sir George Downing, is in fact a folly. Now ruinous and overgrown and standing some 20 feet high, it used to consist of two rusticated piers flanking a large lunette. However, many tales have been passed down about its origin. One such is that it formed part of a wall of the Downing estate and was the letter 'O' of Downing. It is said that the famous highwayman, Dick Turpin, once jumped his horse through the 'O' to evade capture.

GREAT GRANSDEN'S EERIE POST MILL

Position: Great Gransden, 10 miles south of Huntingdon.
Ordnance Map: 1:50,000 Bedford, Huntingdon and surrounding area.
Sheet No: Landranger 153.
Map Reference: 277555.

Access: Take the A14 south from Huntingdon for Royston. At Caxton turn right on to the minor road for Great Gransden. Once in the village take the first juction left and follow straight on to the Mill.

A newspaper cutting from the 1930s relates an interview with Richard Webb of Shefford, Bedfordshire, the grandson of William Webb the last miller at Gransden post mill. His story, which was set in the 1860s, allegedly involved witchcraft. Mrs. Webb, whilst sifting through the belongings of her deceased brother, came upon a book called "The Infidel's Bible", which was all about black magic, a sort of witch's handbook. She was on the point of burning it, when her husband interposed, saying he would sell it when next in town. In spite of his wife's protests and prognostications of bad luck, he took the book and hid it in the mill and forgot all about it. The mill then suddenly stopped working and for three years not a grain of corn was ground in spite of all the efforts of skilled millwrights, who could discover no defect. Webb had to lay off all his men and became almost bankrupt. At this juncture, Richard Webb, the narrator of the story, came to live with his grandparents and heard from his grandmother of the Infidel's Bible. During an exploration of the mill he chanced to find the book and took it home. His grandmother quickly threw the book on the fire. At once the sails began to turn, slowly at first, but with increasing speed as the book was reduced to ashes.

COMMUNAL BAKEHOUSE

Position: Papworth St. Agnes, 4 miles south of Godmanchester, 1 mile west of the A14 Godmanchester to Royston road.
Ordnance Map: 1:50,000 Bedford, Huntingdon and surrounding area.
Sheet No: Landranger 153.
Map Reference: 268646.

Access: Take the A14 from Godmanchester to Royston. After approximately four miles turn right onto minor road signposted Graveley. After a further one mile turn left for Papworth St. Agnes. The bakehouse is on a small green at the entrance to the village.

This 19th century communal bakehouse, constructed circa 1850 from white gault brick with slated roof, is unique in Cambridgeshire. The east end is pedimented and the west end has a tall industrial chimney. The interior of the building, which, apart from baking dough, is said to have been also used for scalding pigs, has been altered. The oven has long since been removed. Built into one wall of the bakehouse is a Victorian letterbox, which is still in use.

MEMORIAL LAMP-POST

Position: In front of 'The Duncombe Arms' public house, Waresley, 9 miles
south of Huntingdon.
Ordnance Map: 1:50,000 Bedford, Huntingdon and surrounding area.
Sheet No: Landranger 153.
Map Reference: 250546.

Access: Take the A1198, formerly the A14, from Huntingdon to Royston. At the
outskirts of Papworth Everard turn left on to the B1040 for Eltisley. At the junction
with the A45(T) turn right then next left back onto the B1040 for Waresley. The
lamp-post is opposite the church at the juction to great Gransden.

The lamp-post was erected in
1897 by the inhabitants of
Waresley to commemorate the
60th year of Queen Victoria's
reign. Originally it was lit by
gas but in 1935 it was
converted to electricity to
celebrate the Silver Jubilee of
their Majesties King George
and Queen Mary. The actual
lamp and glass are now mising,
having been removed during
celebrations of Queen Elizabeth
II's Coronation, it is said, by an
over-enthusiastic Russian
Prince, who once lived at
Waresley. Others say the
removal took place during or
just after the war, but everyone
agrees it was the Russian
Prince.

WARESLEY WATER FOUNTAIN

Position: Opposite 'The Duncombe Arms' public house, Waresley, 9 miles south of Huntingdon.

Ordnance Map: 1:50,000 Bedford, Huntingdon and surrounding area.

Sheet No: Landranger 153.

Map Reference: 249546.

Access: Take the A1198, formerly the A14, from Huntingdon to Royston. At the outskirts of Papworth Everard turn left on to the B1040 for Eltisley. At the junction with the A45(T) turn right then left back on to the B1040 for Waresley. The fountain is in front of the church at the junction to Great Gransden.

Waresley, formerly an 'estate village', contains a varied collection of distinguished houses and cottages of the 19th century, many being thatched and of brick. The Duncombe Arms recalls the name of the family responsible, and itself is a fine example of what a village inn should look like. The old church stood at the eastern end of the village where the churchyard remains in which is a tall cross to remind visitors of the fact. A new church was built opposite the Duncombe Arms by the architect Butterfield in 1857, on the north side of which is the Duncombe mortuary chapel. In front of this church is a delightful wooden pump and stone font, which bears the inscription:

Whosoever Drinketh of the Water shall Thirst Again:
But Whosoever Drinketh of the Water that I shall give him shall never thirst.

THE GOTHIC TOWER

Position: In the grounds of Wimpole Hall, 7 miles north of Royston.
Ordnance Map: 1:50,000 Cambridge, Newmarket and surrounding area.
Sheet No: Landranger 154.
Map Reference: 333521.

Access: Take the A1198 from Royston for Huntingdon. After 5 miles turn right on to the A603 for New Wimpole. After 1½ miles turn left on to minor road signposted for Wimpole Hall. After a further 1½ miles there is a track on the left which goes to the Tower.

The Gothic Tower was first planned by Lord Chancellor Hardwicke on the model of Sanderson Miller's Gothic Castle at Hagley in Worcestershire, built in 1747. In 1749, George Lyttleton, the owner of Hagley, wrote to Miller informing him of Hardwicke's wish to have a replica built at Wimpole. Shortly after Miller visited Wimpole and plans were drawn up, which still survive in the house. However, the project was postponed and it was not until 1768 that the building was finally erected by the 2nd Earl of Hardwicke, under Capability Brown's supervision. Built of brick and rubble, faced with clunch, which has weathered badly, it consists of three circular towers connected by two lengths of curtain wall facing south. The central tower is carried up four storeys and pierced with two-light windows and cross-shaped embrasures. Only fragments of the other towers were built. Above the north door of the middle tower is a mitred head from a medieval statue, possibly 14th century, and a bogus Roman inscription: *STIRKEIVS ABBA CROYLANDIE AD 946 FVNDATOR ACADEMIARVM CANTABRIGIE ET STANDFORDIE* which commemorates Stirkeius, Abbot of Croyland and founder of Cambridge University in AD 946.

15th-CENTURY VILLAGE CROSS

Position: Opposite the Parish Church of Stretham, 10 miles north of Cambridge on the A10(T).
Ordnance Map: 1:50,000 Ely, Wisbech and surrounding area.
Sheet No: Landranger 143.
Map Reference: 513746.

Access: Take the A10(T) north from Cambridge for Ely. At the roundabout with the A1123, Stretham is signposted to the right. The stone market-cross is in the old market place on Akeman Street.

At the time of the Reformation there were probably not less than 5000 crosses in England in the classes of Preaching Crosses, Churchyard Crosses, Memorial Crosses, Market Crosses, etc. The most rudimentary form of cross was a menhir, or vertical monolith, which were still being erected as late as the 12th century as Christian crosses, a good example can be found at Elton.

The next stage in the development of crosses, in use up until the 16th century, for use not only as churchyard crosses but also on village greens or by the wayside, was that of the shaft-on-steps type. The shaft was more of a tapering stem placed on steps and with a cross at the top usually adorned with figures and other ornamentation. The cross surmounting the shaft, known as the head, was the chief target for the despoilers of the Reformation. The restored 15th-century cross at Stretham is a good example of this type of cross. It has an octagonal base with a quatrefoil frieze, a tapering shaft and a cross head with four flat arched niches.

A fair, known as the Stretham feast, was formerly held in the street between the rectory gate and the cross. Older inhabitants used to refer to it as Stretham Pont Feast, because one of the habitual stallholders was Miss Pont, who sold home-made rock.

WICKEN PUMP

Position: On Pond Green, Wicken, 9 miles from Ely.
Ordnance Map: 1:50,000 Cambridge, Newmarket and surrounding area.
Sheet No: Landranger 154.
Map Reference: 568708.

Access: Take the A10(T) south from Ely for Cambridge. At the junction with the A1123 turn left for Stretham. Continue on the A1123 for Wicken. Pond Green is on the left-hand side of the road in the village.

This is the sole remaining pump in Wicken, although it no longer draws water. The village had three pumps by the 1890s, but a fourth was added for the new council houses in the 1920s. In addition, there used to be a motor-driven pump in Lode Lane near Wicken Fen and the public were invited to use the yard pump owned by Solomon Bailey in Chapel Lane. Smallholders, without their own yard pump, made such frequent use of the public ones, bringing their water-barrows with wooden floats, that they sometimes dried them out in high summer.

BIER HOUSE

Position: On the roadside at Wilburton cemetery. 5 miles south-west of Ely.
Ordnance Map: 1:50,000 Ely, Wisbech and surrounding area.
Sheet No: Landranger 143.
Map Reference: 478749.

Access: Take the A141 from Huntingdon for Chatteris. At the Hartford roundabout take the A1123 for St. Ives. Continue on the A1123 through Needingworth, Bluntisham, Earith and Haddenham. The Bier House is on the right-hand side of the road one mile on from the crossroads in the centre of Haddenham.

Seldom seen these days, even in the remotest villages, the bier, a three- or four-wheeled hand-propelled carriage, was the predecessor of the hearse. Many were housed in the church, some with the local coffin-maker, but a few, probably owned by the parish, had their own bier house. This little brick and tile shed on the roadside at Wilburton cemetery is an example of such a bier house.

MILE POST — ALCONBURY HILL

> *Position:* Alconbury Hill on A1(T), approximately 8 miles due south of Norman Cross.
> *Ordnance Map:* 1:50,000 Peterborough and surrounding area.
> *Sheet No:* Landranger 142.
> *Map Reference:* 186784.

Access: The Mile Post is on the central reservation of A1, opposite the Alconbury House Hotel.

Stone sign posts are rare. The grandest of them all stands in a small enclosure on the central reservation of the A1(T) at Alconbury Hill, where the old Ermine Street used to join the Great North Road. The post has carved hands pointing the way as follows:

(Southern Direction):
To London 64 miles through Huntingdon, Royston & Ware;
To Huntingdon 3 miles;
To London 72 miles through Cambridge;
To Cambridge 21 miles.

(Northern Direction):
To London 68 miles through Buckden, Biggleswade and Hatfield;
To Buckden 7 miles;
To Stilton 7 miles.

A REMARKABLE FEAT OF ENGINEERING

Position: Parish Church, Alconbury, 3 miles north of Huntingdon.
Ordnance Map: 1:50,000 Peterborough and surrounding area.
Sheet No: Landranger 142.
Map Reference: 184761.

Access: Take the A141 from Huntingdon and join the A1(T) north. Exit on to the minor road signposted for the Alconburys and take the first right into Alconbury village. After crossing the hump-back bridge turn left and follow the road, through Maypole Square, up to the parish church. The brass plaque, detailing the feat of engineering, is on the west wall of the nave inside.

The parish church is mostly 13th century, however, its fine broach tower underwent an extraordinary and expensive restoration in 1877 when the tower but not the spire was rebuilt. The latter was propped up on massive baulks of timber while the rest was taken down and built up again. Upon completion the spire was allowed to settle down onto its new walls; fortunately it did not topple over. The brass plaque reads:

TO THE GLORY OF GOD AMEN
THE ENTIRE BASE OF THE TOWER
WAS REBUILDED, THE BELL CHAMBER
AND SPIRE MEANTIME REMAINING
AD 1877

Ewan Christian,	*R. Conway,*
Architect	*Vicar*
Thos Williams	*L. Newton*
Builder	*G. J. Rust*
	Church Wardens

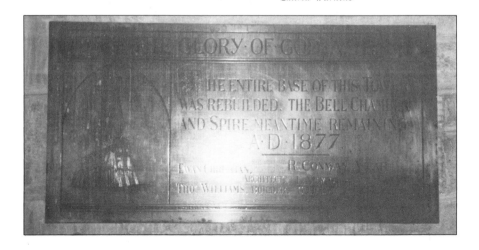

'SANCTUS BELL' WINDOW

Position: St. Mary's Church, Bluntisham, 4 miles east of St. Ives.
Ordnance Map: 1:50,000 Peterborough and surrounding area.
Sheet No: Landranger 142.
Map Reference: 373745.

Access: Take the A141 from Huntingdon for Chatteris. At the Hartford roundabout take the A1123 for St. Ives and then on to Needingworth and Bluntisham.

Low down on the external wall of the south side of the chancel there is a small iron grated opening, once closed by a wooden shutter. Contrary to local opinion these small window openings had nothing to do with lepers, who were not even allowed in the churchyard, but were used for ringing the 'sanctus bell' at certain special moments during the medieval mass, notably the consecration. It should be noted that this opening is on the south side of the church where there are now no houses, thus, at some point in its history, the village must have moved to the more northerly site of today's principal settlement at Block Hill.

BASE OF VILLAGE CROSS

Position: Near to the village green of Brampton, 2 miles from Huntingdon.
Ordnance Map: 1:50,000 Bedford, Huntingdon and surrounding area.
Sheet No: Landranger 153.
Map Reference: 208711.

Access: Take the A141 from Huntingdon to Brampton. At the roundabout situated at the entrance to Brampton village go straight across. Approximately ½ mile further on turn left into Brampton village. The old village cross base is on the right at the bottom of this road near to the village sign.

The 14th-century village cross base was resited in 1972.

BRAMPTON MILE POST

Position: At the roundabout, at the junction of the A604 and A141, in
Brampton village, 2 miles west of Huntingdon.
Ordnance Map: 1:50,000 Bedford, Huntingdon and surrounding area.
Sheet No: Landranger 153.
Map Reference: 215709.

Access: Take the A141 west from Huntingdon for Brampton.

This old mile post is an 18th-
century stone direction obelisk
with hands pointing the way to
Huntingdon, Thrapston and
London. It was dismantled
during World War II in case it
might have given vital
information to the enemy,
should he have had the
temerity to make a parachute
landing and not know where he
was.

THREE SHIRES STONE

Position: On the grass verge of the A45 opposite the water tower at
    Covington, near Kimbolton.
Ordnance Map: 1:50,000 Bedford, Huntingdon and surrounding area.
Sheet No: Landranger 153.
Map Reference: 047705.

Access: Take the A141 from Huntingdon to the A1(T) south. Exit the A1(T), after
approximately 5 miles, on to the A45 for Higham Ferrers. Proceed through Great
Staughton, Kimbolton and Tilbrook. A further 2½ miles on there is a sharp left-
hand bend, opposite a large water tower; the Stone is on the left-hand side of the
road verge.

The Three Shires Stone is an ancient stone which marks the spot where the three
counties of Bedfordshire, Northamptonshire and Huntingdonshire (now part of
Cambridgeshire) all meet. The tall inscribed stone post is a replacement of the
original stone of which it stands atop.

FEN DRAYTON LOCK-UP

Position: Off Horse and Gate Street in Fen Drayton, 6 miles from Huntingdon.
Ordnance Map: 1:50,000 Cambridge, Newmarket and surrounding area.
Sheet No: Landranger 154.
Map Reference: 338681.

Access: Take the A604(T) from Huntingdon for Cambridge and exit for Fen Drayton. Once in the village turn off the High Street into Horse and Gate Street. The lock-up is on the right-hand side of the road as it bends left to the church.

Fen Drayton's lock-up is a good example of one with two cells.

FEN DRAYTON WATER PUMP

Position: Off Horse and Gate Street in Fen Drayton, 6 miles from Huntingdon.
Ordnance Map: 1:50,000 Cambridge, Newmarket and surrounding area.
Sheet No: Landranger 154.
Map Reference: 338682.

Access: Take the A604(T) from Huntingdon for Cambridge and exit for Fen Drayton. Once in the village turn off the High Street into Horse and Gate Street. The Pump is on the left-hand side of the road.

The pump is a typical boxed village hand-pump, which has long since been disused.

VILLAGE LOCK-UP

Position: In the centre of the older part of the village, at the bottom of the High Street, Fenstanton.

Ordnance Map: 1:50,000 Bedford, Huntingdon and surrounding area.

Sheet No: Landranger 153.

Map Reference: 315685.

Access: Take the A604(T) from Cambridge for Huntingdon. Approximately 9 miles from Cambridge, exit on to the minor road for Fenstanton.

Lock-ups were where parish law-breakers were held prior to being taken before the local court. Fenstanton's lock-up, better known as the Clock Tower, is the finest in the county and also the largest suggesting a troublesome village in olden days. The stocks are still kept within its walls. Apart from locking-up miscreants, the building was at one time used to collect market taxes. A plaque on the building reads:

'This clockhouse built circa 1650 was restored May 1989 by Fenstanton Parish Council'.

TOMB OF ENGLAND'S GREATEST GARDENER — LANCELOT 'CAPABILITY' BROWN

Position: On the north side of the chancel, the Church of
St. Peter & Paul, Fenstanton.
Ordnance Map: 1:50,000 Bedford, Huntingdon and surrounding area.
Sheet No: Landranger 153.
Map Reference: 320688.

Access: Take the A604(T) from Cambridge for Huntingdon. Approximately 9 miles from Cambridge, exit on to the minor road for Fenstanton.

Lancelot 'Capability' Brown was born, 1716, in Kirkharle, Northumbria. He became famous as a Landscape Gardener. Many of his creations are still in being. He was also an architect of no mean talent. He was the friend of Kings and the great. He became Lord of the Manor of Fenstanton and Hilton by purchase in 1767. He died in London in February 1783. He lies with his family outside the north side of the chancel. The inscriptions read as follows:

Lancelot Brown Esq died Feb 6th 1783, aged 67 years

Lancelot Brown Esq	*Ye Sons of Elegance, who truly taste*
Son of	*The Simple charms that genuine Art supplies,*
Lancelot & Bridget	*Come from the sylvan Scenes His Genius grace'd*
Brown	*And offer here your tributary Sigh's*
he died 28th Feb 1802	*But know that more than Genius slumbers here,*
in the 54 Year of his	*Virtues were his which Arts best powers transcend*
Age	*Come, ye Superior train who those revere*
	And weep the Christian Husband, Father, Friend

Sacred to the memory of John Brown Esq	*Also sacred to the memory of*
Second Son of	*Mary the Widow of Admiral Brown*
Lancelot & Bridget Brown	*who died March 21st 1834*
An Admiral in the British Navy	*Aged 71 years*
He died the 3rd of May 1808	
Aged 57 years	

Mrs. Bridget Brown
Relict of the above Lancelot Brown Esq
died the 26th of August 1786
Aged 69 Years

LANCELOT BROWN Esq. died Feb. 6, 1783 Aged 67 Years

LANCELOT BROWN Esq.
Son of
LANCELOT & BRIDGET
BROWN
he died the 28 of Feb 1802
in the 54 Year of his
AGE

Ye Sons of Elegance, who truly taste
The Simple charms that genuine Art supply
Come from the gilote Scene He Genius grac'd
And offer here your tributary Sigh's
But know that more than Genius slumbers here
Virtue was which Arts best powers combin'd
·· ·· ·· whofe ·· ··
And ·· the Good ·· Husband ·· ··

Sacred ··
this Memory of JOHN BROWN ··
Second Son of
LANCELOT & BRIDGET ··
An ADMIRAL in the ·· ··
He died the 8 of ··
Aged Years
Also ··
in the Memory of
MARY the WIDOW of
ADMIRAL BROWN
who died ·· of ··
Aged Years

Mrs. BRIDGET BROWN
Relict of the above Lancelot Brown Esq
died the 26 of August 1786
Aged 69 Years

PRE-REFORMATION CLERGY SEATS & COMMUNION 'WASHING-UP SINK'

> *Position:* On the south side of the sanctuary wall, the Church of St. Peter & Paul, Fenstanton.
>
> *Ordnance Map:* 1:50,000 Bedford, Huntingdon and surrounding area.
>
> *Sheet No:* Landranger 153.
>
> *Map Reference:* 320688.

Access: Take A604(T) from Cambridge for Huntingdon. Approximately 9 miles from Cambridge, exit on to the minor road for Fenstanton.

St. Peter & Paul's Church has a fine triple sedilia and piscina. The sedilia were seats used by the clergy in Pre-Reformation times during the singing of the creed or a long sermon. The seats look low because the sanctuary floor was raised considerably in the 19th century. The piscina is where the Communion vessels were washed in the years before the Reformation and the drain goes through the wall to the ground outside.

CHINESE BRIDGE, GODMANCHESTER

Position: Near to the junction of the Causeway and Cambridge Street
in Godmanchester.
Ordnance Map: 1:50,000 Bedford, Huntingdon and surrounding area.
Sheet No: Landranger 153.
Map Reference: 244706.

Access: From the Huntingdon ring road take the B1043 for Godmanchester.

The familiar town bridge at Godmanchester, known as the Chinese Bridge, was built
in 1827 from a design based on the Chinese Bridge at Island Hall, Godmanchester.
The architect was I. Gallier. Since the bridge had to allow boats to pass underneath
it, it was built with a curved rather than a flat walkway which, to cover such a span,
would have necessitated the construction of piers to carry it. The bridge was rebuilt
in 1869. The current replica replacement was provided by the Godmanchester
Borough Council in 1960.

MARIA WEEMS MEMORIAL HEADSTONE

Position: Parish Church, Godmanchester, 1 mile from Huntingdon.
Ordnance Map: 1:50,000 Bedford, Huntingdon and surrounding area.
Sheet No: Landranger 153.
Map Reference: 246707.

Access: Take the B1043, south from Huntingdon, to Godmanchester.

In the churchyard, south east of the chancel, is the replica memorial stone of Maria Weems, murdered by her husband in 1819. The original was broken during tree-lopping. The stone bears the following inscription:

> *To the Memory of Mary Ann*
> *Weems who was murdered*
> *in the 21st year of her age*
> *As a Warning*
> *to the Young of both Sexes*
> *This stone is erected by public subscription*
> *over the remains of Mary Ann Weems*
> *who at an early age became acquainted*
> *with Thomas Weems formerly by this Parish*
> *this connection terminating in a compulsory*
> *Marriage occasioned him soon to desert her*
> *and wishing to be married to another Woman*
> *he filled up the measure of his iniquity*
> *by resolving to murder his wife*
> *which he barbarously perpetrated at Wendy*
> *on their journey to London toward which place*
> *he had induced her to go under the mask*
> *of reconciliation May the 7th 1819.*
> *He was taken within a few hours after*
> *the crime was committed, tried and*
> *subsequently executed at Cambridge*
> *on the 7th August in the same Year.*

Thomas Weems had been seen by a woman tending a sick cow who stopped a coach in which, by luck, was a Justice of the Peace. Pious people, thought the conjunction of the woman witness and the passing Justice a direct intervention of God in discovering and taking the murderer. Thus, at the bottom of the headstone is the following warning epitaph:

> *Ere Crime you perpetrate, survey this Stone*
> *Learn hence the God of Justice sleeps not on his throne*
> *But marks the sinner with unerring eye*
> *The suffering Victim hears and makes the guilty die.*

As a Warning
to the Young of both Sexes
This Stone is erected by public Subscription
over the remains of MARY ANN WEEMS,
who at an early age became acquainted
with THOMAS WEEMS formerly of this Parish
this connexion terminating in a compulfory
Marriage occafioned him foon to defert her
and wifhing to be Married to another Woman
he filled up the measure of his iniquity
by refolving to murder his Wife
which he barbaroufly perpetrated at Wendy
on their journey to London toward which place
he had induced her to go under the mask
of reconciliation May the 7th 1819
He was taken within a few hours after
the crime was committed, tried and
subfequently executed at Cambridge
on the 7th of Auguft in the fame Year

Ere Crime you perpetrate survey this Stone
Learn hence the God of Juftice Sleeps not on his Throne
But marks the Sinner with unerring Eye
The fuffering Victim hears and makes the Guilty die

OLD SCHOOL SUNDIAL, GODMANCHESTER

Position: On the wall of the old school building next to the Chinese Bridge, near the junction of the Causeway and Cambridge Street in Godmanchester.

Ordnance Map: 1:50,000 Bedford, Huntingdon and surrounding area.

Sheet No: Landranger 153.

Map Reference: 245706.

Access: Take the B1043, off the Huntingdon ring road, for Godmanchester.

Next to the 19th-century town hall, no longer used as such, is the Queen Elizabeth Grammar School, founded in 1561, of which the school hall remains. But it never became a grammar school as its founders intended and for many years was an elementary school before the better and newer one was built near the church. Above the open gated porch a sundial is let into the wall and beneath it is written the inscription:

> *Eliz. Reg. Hujus*
> *Scholae Fundatrix*
>
> *Restaurata*
> *MDCCCLI*

The school is small; two separately gabled large rooms form the basic structure, and outside the mellow red brick is built in dog-toothing below the eaves. The roof itself is of hand made tiles and on one gable is the open wooden tower where the school bell still rings. The porch houses the Parish Museum which opens on Sundays from 2.00 — 5.00pm.

ROMAN OBELISK

Position: Parish Church, Hartford, 1 mile from Huntingdon.
Ordnance Map: 1:50,000 Bedford, Huntingdon and surrounding area.
Sheet No: Landranger 153.
Map Reference: 256726.

Access: Hartford is on the outskirts of Huntingdon on the A141 for Chatteris. The parish church stands down by the river.

The parish church of All Saints, which dates from the 12th century, was drastically treated by Victorian restorers, nevertheless it has a fine picturesque tower. By the south east angle of the chancel is a stone obelisk inscribed 'Mors Meta Viarum' and the date 1735 in Roman numerals. The translation is as follows:

Death is the turning point of the ways.

This is a pun on the Roman word 'meta' or stone marking where chariots turned during races and it refers to the clearing of the churchyard so it could be buried over again; there were no cemeteries in those days.

HILTON TURF MAZE

Position: At Hilton, approximately 6 miles south-east of Huntingdon on
the B1040, which runs between two old Roman roads, the A14,
Ermine Street, and the A604(T), the Via Devana.

Ordnance Map: 1:50,000 Bedford, Huntingdon and surrounding area.

Sheet No: Landranger 153.

Map Reference: 295663.

Access: Take A14 from Huntingdon to Godmanchester. Remain on A14 and head
towards Royston. After approximately 4 miles take minor road on left signposted
Hilton. In Hilton at crossroads with B1040 go straight across heading towards
Fenstanton. The maze is located on The Green.

Hilton Maze, or Labyrinth, is one of only eight surviving turf mazes in England.
According to the Latin inscription on the Monument in the centre, it was cut in
1660, the year of Charles II's Restoration, by William Sparrow (1541-1729), who
lived in a house on the site of Park Farm opposite where a painting of the Royal
Arms, now in Hilton church, was found. He probably copied the pattern of the
Maze, often found in medieval art, most notably in Chartres Cathedral, from a maze,
now destroyed, at Comberton, 11 miles away, where his brother-in-law, Baron
Brittaine, lived.

Little is known of the origin of mazes but they are believed to have been used in
fertility rites and to cast out the Devil, who was reputed to go only in a straight
line. By following the Labyrinth out from the centre the Devil could be left behind
and his influences overcome. Turf mazes were once common on village greens, but
they disappear if neglected as Shakespeare implies in 'A Midsummer Night's Dream':

> And the quaint mazes in the wanton green
> For lack of tread are indistinguishable.

The Maze is scheduled as an Ancient Monument and is the responsibility of Hilton
Parish Council.

HOLY WELL

Position: In the churchyard at Holywell near Needingworth, 6 miles east of Huntingdon.

Ordnance Map: 1:50,000 Cambridge, Newmarket and surrounding area.

Sheet No: Landranger 154.

Map Reference: 337708.

Access: Take the A141 from Huntingdon for Chatteris. At the Hartford roundabout take the A1123 for St. Ives and then Needingworth. In Needingworth turn right for Holywell and follow the road down to the church.

Just below the church is the "holy well" from which the village takes its name. Here is a spring which must have attained a sanctity in heathen times which could not be eradicated when Christianity was introduced into England and was "converted" by having the church built close to it. Little is known of its history but it had a reputation for curing sore eyes. Also, it is recorded that in much later times, unmarried maidens resorted to it, threw money into the water, and then hoped to see the reflection of the man they would marry. Both these traditions point to a heathen origin. The spring retained its health-giving reputation down to the early 19th century, when a brick canopy was built over it to keep the water clear of weeds and leaves. The canopy was erected by the Rev. S. B. Beckwith, rector of the parish, in 1845.

THE GHOST OF JULIET TEWSLEY

Position: Ye Olde Ferryboat Inn, Holywell near Needingworth, 6 miles east of Huntingdon.

Ordnance Map: 1:50,000 Cambridge, Newmarket and surrounding area.

Sheet No: Landranger 154.

Map Reference: 342707.

Access: Take the A141 from Huntingdon for Chatteris. At the Hartford roundabout take the A1123 for St. Ives and then Needingworth. In Needingworth turn right for Holywell and follow the road down to the river and the Inn.

Ye Olde Ferryboat Inn, which dates back to the 11th century, claims to be the oldest pub in England. It is renowned for its ghost, that of Juliet Tewsley. Back in 1050 lovesick Juliet committed suicide because of her unrequited love for the local woodcutter, Thomas Zoul, who spurned her affections in preference for ale and ninepins. She hanged herself from a tree beside the river and, therefore, because her death was by suicide, was buried on unconsecrated ground at nearby crossroads. Her body was allegedly moved and today the gravestone is a feature in the inn's lounge. Ever since Juliet's ghost has haunted the pub and numerous sightings have been reported on the anniversary of her death, the 17th March. The last lengthy scientific investigation of the Ferryboat ghost was in 1953, by a team from the Society for Physical Research headed by an American psychic, Tony Cornell, and according to a newspaper report of the investigation a medium made contact.

SITE OF ST. BENEDICT'S CHURCH

Position: Shopping Precinct, High Street, Huntingdon.
Ordnance Map: 1:50,000 Bedford, Huntingdon and surrounding area.
Sheet No: Landranger 153.
Map Reference: 239717.

Access: The gazebo is situated opposite Chequer's Court in the High Street, Huntingdon.

The gazebo, centred in Huntingdon's shopping precinct, was built with stone from, and stands on the site of, St. Benedict's Church, which was damaged beyond repair when Charles I entered Huntingdon in 1645. The columns were cast in Huntingdon and originally supported the roof of the Meat Market in Princes Street.

THE OLD BRIDGE, GODMANCHESTER/HUNTINGDON

Position: On the B1043, which crosses the Ouse River and which links
     Huntingdon and Godmanchester.
Ordnance Map: 1:50,000 Bedford, Huntingdon and surrounding area.
Sheet No: Landranger 153.
Map Reference: 243715.

Access: Exit Huntingdon ring road for Godmanchester. The B1043 crosses the
river Ouse.

This old 14th-century bridge is a good example of 'by guess and by God'
construction. The bridge has been constructed with a slight curve, which was not
deliberately intended. This is because construction commenced at opposite ends of
the river bank without either side working to a co-ordinated plan. Thus, in order to
make the two ends meet in the middle a slight curve had to be introduced.

POTTO BROWN MEMORIAL

Position: In the corner of the village green, near to the thatched shelter, of
Houghton & Wyton midway between St. Ives and Huntingdon on
the A1123.
Ordnance Map: 1:50,000 Bedford, Huntingdon and surrounding area.
Sheet No: Landranger 153.
Map Reference: 282722.

Access: Take the A141 from Huntingdon for Chatteris. At the roundabout just past
Hartford turn right on to the A1123 for St. Ives. Exit right after 1 mile for
Houghton & Wyton.

Potto Brown, a Quaker
merchant and nonconformist,
was also a philanthropist who
built a school and
Nonconformist chapel in the
village in 1840. Potto leased
Houghton Mill, in 1822, from
Lady Olivia Bernard Sparrow, a
High Church Anglican of the
locality, and worked it with his
partner, Joseph Goodman, until
he retired in 1862, when his
son Bateman carried on the
business for another 14 years.
The bust bears the inscription:

*Potto Brown was born in this
village 18 July 1797 where he spent
his life devoting himself to the best
interests of those around him, and
died 12 April 1871*

THOMAS GARNER'S HEADSTONE

Position: St. Mary's churchyard, Houghton & Wyton situated midway between St. Ives and Huntingdon on the A1123.
Ordnance Map: 1:50,000 Bedford, Huntingdon and surrounding area.
Sheet No: Landranger 153.
Map Reference: 282721.

Access: Take the A141 from Huntingdon for Chatteris. At the roundabout just past Hartford turn right on to the A1123 for St. Ives. Exit right after 1 mile for Houghton & Wyton. At the village square, with its picturesque thatched shelter turn right down Church Lane towards Houghton Mill and St. Mary's Church.

Close by the south porch is the restored headstone of Thomas Garner, the village blacksmith who died in 1826. It bears the inscription:

> *My sledge and hammers lie declined*
> *My bellows too have lost their wind*
> *My fire's extinct, my forge decayed*
> *My vice is in the dust all laid*
> *My nails are drove, my work is done*
> *My fire-dried corpse here lies at rest*
> *My soul smoke-like, soars to be blest.*

Thomas Garner lived in a house by the village green. The ends of the tie-rods in the roof, normally 'X' or 'S' are 'T' and 'G' shaped.

HOUGHTON MILL

Position: On the bank of the river Ouse at Houghton & Wyton midway
between St. Ives and Huntingdon on the A1123.
Ordnance Map: 1:50,000 Bedford, Huntingdon and surrounding area.
Sheet No: Landranger 153.
Map Reference: 282720.

Access: Take the A141 from Huntingdon for Chatteris. At the roundabout just past
Hartford turn right on to the A1123 for St. Ives. Exit right after 1 mile for
Houghton & Wyton. In the village square turn right down Church Lane to the Mill.

Houghton Water Corn Mill belongs to the National Trust. It is one of the last and
most complete to survive along the river Ouse. A mill has been on this site for at
least 1000 years but much of the present mill dates from the 17th century when it
replaced an earlier one destroyed by fire. The mill is a rectangular building of brick,
partly timber-framed and covered with weather boarding. Originally the roof would
have been thatched but this has been replaced by slates. Various extensions have also
been made to the building in the 18th and 19th centuries. In 1930 the mill ceased
working and its fate hung in the balance for a time until it was bought and given to
the National Trust. It was initially leased by the Trust to the Youth Hostels
Association, but today is open to members of the public.

ALABASTER TOMBS OF THE TYRWHITT FAMILY

Position: St. Mary's Church, Leighton Bromswold.
Ordnance Map: 1:50,000 Peterborough and surrounding area.
Sheet No: Landranger 142.
Map Reference: 115753.

Access: Exit A1(T) northbound on to A604 for Kettering. After bypassing the villages of Ellington and Spaldwick, both on the left, take minor road approximately 1 mile further on, to the right for Leighton Bromswold.

Leighton Bromswold's Church of St. Mary is one of the most interesting in this part of England, particularly because it contains a magnificent collection of 17th-century woodwork, which was largely due to the Rev. George Herbert, Vicar of Bemerton near Salisbury, who held the living but probably never visited the church. In about 1606 he replaced the aisled nave and using the fine 13th-century entrance doorways as the outer arches for the porches he built. The work was completed in 1626. Also of note are the alabaster tombs of Sir Robert Tyrwhitt, who died 1572, his wife Elizabeth (nee Oxenbridge), who died 1578, and daughter Katherine, who died 1567 and was the wife of Sir Henry D'Arcy. Sir Robert's wife, Elizabeth, was Governess of Queen Elizabeth I and Maid-of-Honour to Catherine Parr, the surviving wife of King Henry VIII.

LEIGHTON HUNDRED STONE

Position: In front of St. Mary's Church, Leighton Bromswold.
Ordnance Map: 1:50,000 Peterborough and surrounding area.
Sheet No: Landranger 142.
Map Reference: 115753.

Access: Exit A1(T) northbound on to A604 for Kettering. After bypassing the villages of Ellington and Spaldwick, both on the left, take the minor road approximately 1 mile further on, on the right for Leighton Bromswold. The Hundred stone is located in front of St. Mary's Church at the junction of Church Lane, Sheep Street and The Avenue.

The stone thought to be about a thousand years old represents the ancient seat of judgement. It was placed in the centre of an area of 100 units where taxes were collected and criminals of the day were brought to judgement. There were four of these in Huntingdonshire: Leighton (stone), Hursting (stone), Toseland and Norman Cross. At one time the stone was situated at the other side of the church but was removed to this side.

THE SIGN OF THE OLD SWAN AND SALMON INN

Position: Opposite Church Way, Little Stukeley, 3 miles from Huntingdon.
Ordnance Map: 1:50,000 Peterborough and surrounding area.
Sheet No: Landranger 142.
Map Reference: 209755.

Access: Take the B1043 north from Huntingdon towards the Stukeleys. After passing through Great Stukeley, Little Stukeley is encountered. Directly opposite Church Way, which is on the right-hand side of the road, is the former inn.

The former Swan and Salmon Inn, now a private house, was built in 1676. Its presence as an Inn was advertised by the attractive plaster plaque that survives on the gable-end of the building.

THE TOMBSTONE OF THE UNLUCKY RECTOR

Position: Parish Church of St. Martin, Little Stukeley, 3 miles from Huntingdon.
Ordnance Map: 1:50,000 Peterborough and surrounding area.
Sheet No: Landranger 142.
Map Reference: 209757.

Access: Take the B1043 north from Huntingdon towards the Stukeleys. After passing through Great Stukeley, Little Stukeley is encountered. In the village, turn right into Church Way. The table-tomb of the Reverend Waterhouse is to the left of the entrance gate to St. Martin's Church.

The Reverend Joshua Waterhouse was murdered by his house-boy in 1827. His table-tomb bears the following very badly worn epitaph:

Beneath this tomb his mangled body's laid,
Cut, stabb'd and murdered by Joshua Slade,
His ghastly wounds a horrid sight to see,
And hurl'd at once into Eternity.

What faults you've seen in him take care to shun
And look at home — enough there's to be done
Death does not allways warning give
Therefore be carefull how you live.

The rector was apparently a very difficult person in every way and this so upset Slade that he murdered him and put his body in a bran tub. It was some time before the murderer was found, hiding in a culvert at the bottom of the hill between Great and Little Stukeley. He was tried at Huntingdon Assizes and subsequently executed. The Rev. Waterhouse was also an eccentric and directed in his will that he should be buried 18 feet down and with his favourite horse beside him — a request that was not carried out.

NEEDINGWORTH LOCK-UP

Position: Junction of High Street and Overcote Lane, Needingworth.
Ordnance Map: 1:50,000 Cambridge, Newmarket and surrounding area.
Sheet No: Landranger 154.
Map Reference: 343721.

Access: Take the A141 from Huntingdon for Chatteris. At the Hartford roundabout take the A1123 for St. Ives. Continue on through St. Ives into Needingworth. The lock-up is on the right-hand side of the High Street, near to the Queen's Head public house.

The large hamlet of Needingworth is in the parish of Holywell and one mile from the church. It was almost completely burnt down in a great fire on September 16, 1847, and was rebuilt in a very plain and uninteresting manner. A map in the church shows the extent of the damage. Consequently, there is little of interest to the visitor, however, Needingworth does retain its lock-up, built in 1838, on the corner of the road leading down to the Pike and Eel Inn on the river bank about a mile away.

THE BRIDGE CHAPEL OF ST. LEGER

Position: The old bridge spanning the River Great Ouse at St. Ives, 5 miles east of Huntingdon.

Ordnance Map: 1:50,000 Bedford, Huntingdon and surrounding area.

Sheet No: Landranger 153.

Map Reference: 313712.

Access: Take the A141 from Huntingdon for Chatteris. At the Hartford roundabout take the A1123 for St. Ives.

The 15th-century stone-built bridge spans the River Great Ouse with six arches, from the southern end of Bridge Street and is one of three surviving bridges in the country. The structure was rebuilt in 1716 when Charles, 1st Duke of Manchester replaced the southern two arches, which had been dismantled and replaced with a wooden drawbridge section during the English Civil War. The Chapel of St. Leger stands above the central pier and was built as a place of worship for passing travellers. It was converted into a small dwelling in 1736 when two additional storeys were added but were removed in 1930. Inside, the chapel has simple wooden furnishings and a railed balcony that overlooks the river and quayside. The Chapel is open all year round and admission is free.

THE HURSTINGSTONE OR "ABBOT'S CHAIR"

Position: The Norris Museum, St. Ives, 5 miles east of Huntingdon.
Ordnance Map: 1:50,000 Bedford, Huntingdon and surrounding area.
Sheet No: Landranger 153.
Map Reference: 312714.

Access: Take the A141 from Huntingdon for Chatteris. At the Hartford roundabout take the A1123 for St. Ives.

This stone originally formed the base of a wayside cross. It was erected, perhaps in the 12th or 13th century, on the road from St. Ives to Old Hurst. The road is now cut by the main runway of RAF Wyton, at about the spot where the stone used to stand. On a map of 1725 it was recorded as the "Psalm Stone".

The Hurstingstone was used as a meeting place of the Hundred Court. A "Hundred" was a medieval administrative area consisting of a group of parishes, and the Hurstingstone Hundred included St. Ives, Huntingdon and Ramsey. It was quite usual in those days for a court to meet in the open air.

The stone is known locally as "The Abbot's Chair", because of its shape. Legend has it that monks stopped to rest in the Chair when travelling between Ramsey Abbey and St. Ives Priory. It is said that if the stone ever sinks below ground, blood will flow in the streets of Bluntisham. Bloodstains are supposed to be visible on the stone, and a ghost is said to haunt it.

FAMOUS EPITAPH

Position: In the churchyard of the parish church, St. Ives, 5 miles east of Huntingdon.

Ordnance Map: 1:50,000 Bedford, Huntingdon and surrounding area.

Sheet No: Landranger 153.

Map Reference: 310716.

Access: Take the A141 from Huntingdon for Chatteris. At the Hartford roundabout take the A1123 for St. Ives. At the traffic lights in St. Ives turn right into Ramsey Road, then take the second right into Westwood Road followed by the first left into Church Street, at the top of which is St. George's Church. The headstone to John Francis is in the churchyard.

The headstone bears the famous epitaph to John Edwards who died in 1822:

A crumb of Jacob's dust lies here below
Richer than all the mines of Mexico
Its lying in the ruins does not prove
The Lord's neglect nor the decay of love
It ever was and always is his delight
It ne'er was moved one moment from his sight
'Twill rise and shine till Nature's time is o'er
Bright on the Firmament for evermore.

The headstone is carved with an urn from which rises a column of smoke and near it is an angel in the sky restraining a man with a large sword from beheading a kneeling boy; a depiction of the sacrifice of Abraham.

87

ST. IVES MILEPOST

Position: At the roundabout junction of the B1040 and the A1123, St. Ives.
Ordnance Map: 1:50,000 Bedford, Huntingdon and surrounding area.
Sheet No: Landranger 153.
Map Reference: 322722.

Access: Take the A141 from Huntingdon for Chatteris. At the Hartford roundabout take the A1123 for St. Ives. Continue on through St. Ives to the first of two roundabouts. The sign is on the verge of this roundabout.

At the junction with the Somersham Road, near Stocks Bridge, is the restored 'White Post' of 1772 rebuilt on its original site when Republic Cottage, an old toll-bar house, was removed for road widening. It was discovered in two pieces doing duty as gate posts of the back entrance to the cottage and was replaced by the County Surveyor. This mile post is one of a pair; the other is located at the Somersham end of the B1040. The tall, slimly-tapered stone's hands point the way, on three of its four sides, to St. Ives and London, to Earith and Ely, and to Somersham, Chatteris, March and Wisbech.

STONE COFFIN

Position: The Norris Museum, St. Ives, 5 miles east of Huntingdon.
Ordnance Map: 1:50,000 Bedford, Huntingdon and surrounding area.
Sheet No: Landranger 153.
Map Reference: 312714.

Access: Take the A141 from Huntingdon for Chatteris. At the Hartford roundabout take the A1123 for St. Ives.

The coffin, found at Water Newton, dates from Roman times, probably the 3rd or 4th century A.D. Water Newton, nowadays just a village in north Huntingdonshire, was then the site of the Roman town of DVROBRIVAE, which stood on the main road from London to York, with an important pottery industry.

The coffin was quarried at Barnack, a few miles away from Water Newton across the River Nene. Barnack's superb limestone was used for many buildings in Huntingdonshire and beyond until the quarries were exhausted in the 18th century.

WOODHURST VILLAGE PUMP

Position: Next to St. John's Close, Woodhurst, north of Huntingdon.
Ordnance Map: 1:50,000 Peterborough and surrounding area.
Sheet No: Landranger 142.
Map Reference: 316761.

Access: Take the A141 north from Huntingdon for Chatteris. After passing Wyton Airfield turn right on to the minor road for Woodhurst.

A fine restored boxed hand-pump with splash guard. Of note is the village church opposite.

RUINS OF ST. MARY'S CHURCH, WOOLLEY

Position: Next to The Manor House in Woolley.
Ordnance Map: 1:50,000 Peterborough and surrounding area.
Sheet No: Landranger 142.
Map Reference: 149745.

Access: Exit from the A1(T) northbound on to the minor road signposted Woolley approximately 1 mile after the roundabout at the junction of A604 for Kettering and A141 for Brampton.

The church is not mentioned in the Domesday Survey 1086 but many 12th century stones built into the wall suggests the church was there at the time. The chancel, nave and transepts were built c1300 and various extensions and restoration work carried out over the centuries. The last service in the registers was on 29th September 1949. Due to the decline in the population and the dangerous state of the roof, St. Mary's was formally closed and finally demolished in 1961-2. The Parish of Woolley was then united with the Parish of Barham. In the churchyard are the ruins of the Church, old tombstones and some graves; it is still open for burials.

In 1618 the living of St. Mary's was given to one Mikepher Alphery, who attained notoriety as it was said he was born in Russia of the Imperial line. He is supposed to have come to England as a boy for safety during a revolt in his own land and joined the family of Mr. Bedell, a Russian Merchant. Later he went to Oxford University subsequently taking Holy Orders. His wife was buried in the churchyard in 1655 and her grave can still be found.

In 1643, during the Civil War, he was thrown out by Puritan reformers while conducting a service and forced from the living. He went to live at Hammersmith where he stayed until after the Restoration when he returned to Woolley. But being over 80 years old he employed a curate to undertake the parochial duties and died shortly afterwards in 1688.

A bell given to Woolley by Mikepher Alphery can now be seen in Barham Church, together with a small Altar and a fine Triptych, that is, a three panelled Altar piece. The Church Plate, consisting of a Silver Chalice and cover dated 1577/8 is kept in safe custody and used once or twice a year at Barham.

HOLME FEN POST

Position: Holme Fen, near Holme, 4 miles south of the Norman Cross
roundabout on the A1(T).
Ordnance Map: 1:50,000 Peterborough and surrounding area.
Sheet No: Landranger 142.
Map Reference: 203893.

Access: Take the A1(T) north from Huntingdon. Approximately 6 miles past the
Alconbury House Hotel, turn right on to the B660 for Holme. Turn left, on to the
minor road for Yaxley, just before the railway crossing. Then take the first turning
right onto a narrow single-track road and cross the main east coast railway line. Park
at the third lay-by along this road. The 'Post' is on the opposite side of the Holme
Lode which runs parallel to the road.

The Holme Fen Post, a cast iron pillar from the Crystal Palace Exhibition, was
erected in 1851 on the south-west edge of Whittlesey Mere. It replaced the wooden
posts which had been erected in 1848 to indicate peat shrinkage caused by drainage.
The post was driven 22 feet through the peat, into buttery clay, until its top was
flush with the ground. Within 10 years the ground level had fallen nearly five feet
through shrinkage. A second post was erected, in 1957, with its top at the same level
as that of the original post. Plaques fixed to this post show the ground levels at
various succeeding dates, namely, 1848, 1860, 1870, 1875 and 1892. As one stands by
the pillar now, on peat that actually quivers underfoot, it is difficult to realise men
who watched the last of the Mere, 120 years ago stood level with its top nearly 13
feet above today's ground level.

HOLME SCHOOL INSCRIPTION

Position: On the wall of Holme School, 10 miles north of Huntingdon.
Ordnance Map: 1:50,000 Peterborough and surrounding area.
Sheet No: Landranger 142.
Map Reference: 189879.

Access: Take the A1(T) north from Huntingdon. Approximately 6 miles past the Alconbury House Hotel, turn right on to the B660 for Holme. After approximately one-and-a-half miles turn left into Holme village. The school is on the right-hand side of the road.

Holme is a pretty fenland village of thatched cottages alongside the main King's Cross railway south of Peterborough. The school wall bears the following inscription:

> *The School Van having been started in 1877*
> *by William Wells, of Holme Wood, to carry*
> *the little Fen children to and from school*
> *in the winter months. Lady Louisa Wells is*
> *anxious that it should be kept up in memory*
> *of her dear husband in this place always,*
> *And for this purpose she gives and bequeaths*
> *the required sum. 1891.*

Also of note in the village is the church, largely rebuilt in 1862, which is unusual for its double dovecote.

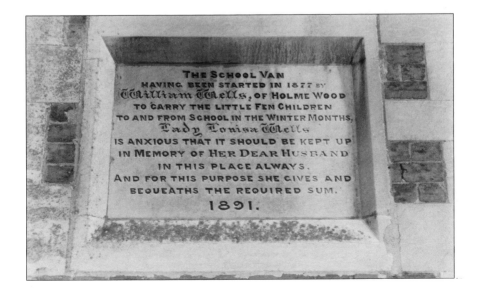

WAR MEMORIAL

Position: On the A1(T) near Norman Cross.
Ordnance Map: 1:50,000 Peterborough and surrounding area.
Sheet No: Landranger 142.
Map Reference: 158914.

Access: Take the A1(T) north from Huntingdon. The war memorial is on the verge of the north bound carriageway just after the Norman Cross roundabout at the junction of the A1(T) and the A15 to Peterborough.

The memorial, which was presented by the Entente Cordiale Society to the County of Huntingdon, was unveiled by the Right Hon. The Baron Weardale, President of the Society, on 27 July 1914. The plain 20 foot column is surmounted by an eagle. At the base of the column a plaque commemorates:

> ONE THOUSAND SEVEN HUNDRED & SEVENTY
> SOLDIERS AND SAILORS
> NATIVES OR ALLIES OF FRANCE
> TAKEN PRISONERS OF WAR DURING THE
> REPUBLICAN AND NAPOLEONIC WARS
> WITH GREAT BRITAIN AD *1793-1814*
> WHO DIED IN THE MILITARY DEPOT
> AT NORMAN CROSS, WHICH FORMERLY
> STOOD NEAR THIS SPOT, *1797-1814*
> DVLCE . ET . DECORVM . EST . PRO . PATRIA . MORI

Although the prison has long since gone, the Commandant's house, three storeyed with parapet walls and bays, still stands on the road to Yaxley.

WANSFORD BRIDGE

Position: Wansford, 6 miles west of Peterborough.
Ordnance Map: 1:50,000 Peterborough and surrounding area.
Sheet No: Landranger 142.
Map Reference: 077989.

Access: Take the A47(T) west from Peterborough. After crossing the A1(T) turn left into Wansford.

Wansford bridge crosses the River Nene, which was liable to sudden flooding. Passers-by on the bridge were surprised one morning to find a local rustic floating underneath it on a hayrick. He had fallen asleep and the rick had been swept up in the floodwater. "Where am I?" cried the poor fellow, not knowing how long he had slept or how far he had travelled. "You are at Wansford," came the reply. "What, Wansford in England?" he asked. And the village has been labelled 'Wansford in England' ever since. The sign on the Haycock Inn features the rustic from the story.

GATEHOUSE AND LANTERN

Position: Down Hall Farm, Abington Pigotts, 4 miles north-west of Royston.
Ordnance Map: 1:50,000 Bedford, Huntingdon and surrounding area.
Sheet No: Landranger 153.
Map Reference: 304437.

Access: Take A14 north from Royston. After approximately three miles take minor road on left signposted Bassingbourn and Litlington. At Litlington follow signs for Abington Pigotts. After 1 mile turn left on to 'no through road' for Down Hall Farm.

Down Hall gatehouse is a 15th century, smooth stuccoed, timber-framed gatehouse which stands behind the moat. It is topped by an enclosed lantern, which was used as a guide for the benefit of travellers venturing across the Moor.

ARRINGTON ALMSHOUSES

Position: In Arrington, 6 miles from Royston.
Ordnance Map: 1:50,000 Bedford, Huntingdon and surrounding area.
Sheet No: Landranger 153.
Map Reference: 328503.

Access: Take the A1198, formerly the A14, from Huntingdon for Royston. The almshouses are on the left-hand side of the road in Arrington, 7 miles on from the Caxton Gibbet roundabout.

The six almshouses were erected in 1846 by Susan, 4th Countess of Hardwicke, in memory of her mother, and now belong to the National Trust. They are constructed from red brick with stone dressings in the Tudor manner. They consist of a one-storey range fronting the road and two-storey wings projecting to the east, with central porch and subsidiary porches in the angles. They were designed by H. E. Kendall. The six houses are now four dwellings numbered 123, 125, 127 and 129. At the back of the houses in a small yard is a communal bakehouse. Inside the central porch an inscribed stone reads:

To the memory of a beloved mother whose example prompted the feeling and whose affection furnished the means. These alms houses are erected by Susan 4th Countess of Hardwicke in the year of our Lord 1846.

Support ye the weak: remember the words of the Lord Jesus how he said it is more blessed to give than to receive. Acts. XX. 35.

OLD MALTHOUSE

Position: No. 13 High Street, Foxton, approximately 6 miles north-east of Royston.

Ordnance Map: 1:50,000 Cambridge, Newmarket and surrounding area.

Sheet No: Landranger 154.

Map Reference: 408481.

Access: Take the A10(T) from Royston for Cambridge. After passing through Melbourn, two miles further, turn right for Foxton. The Old Malthouse is approximately ½ mile further on, on the left hand side, opposite Caxton Lane and near to The Green.

Malthouses were once a common sight in the days when alehouses brewed their own beer. Sadly, many have disappeared and nowadays one has to travel far afield to find one. This malthouse, which dates from the 18th century, was converted as many others have been, into a private dwelling in 1870. Almost opposite the malthouse is a Victorian letterbox.

POST MILL

Position: On the B1039 between Barley, and Great Chishill, approximately
    4 miles south-east of Royston.
Ordnance Map: 1:50,000 Cambridge, Newmarket and surrounding area.
Sheet No: Landranger 154.
Map Reference: 413388.

Access: From Royston take the B1039 for Barley. At the crossroads with the B1368
go straight across for Great Chishill. The Post Mill is on the right-hand side of the
road, approximately 1 mile on from these crossroads.

The Post Mill is an interesting example of rural engineering and is scheduled as an
historic monument. It was built in 1810 using timbers from an earlier mill of 1726
and last worked in 1951. It was restored in 1966 by R. Thompson & Son,
Millwrights of Alford, Lincs. The mill is open to the general public from 1st April
to 31st October, and the key can be obtained from Mrs. A. Coxall, 12 Wallers Close,
Gt. Chishill (off Hall Lane).

LOCK-UP, LITLINGTON

Position: On village green at junction of Middle Street and Meeting Lane, Litlington, near Royston.
Ordnance Map: 1:50,000 Bedford, Huntingdon and surrounding area.
Sheet No: Landranger 153.
Map Reference: 312428.

Access: Take A14 north from Royston. After approximately three miles take minor road on left signposted Bassingbourn and Litlington. At Litlington follow the one-way street system around into Meeting Lane.

Most villages had somewhere where miscreants could contemplate their sins, await transport to the County Gaol or sober up. Litlington was no exception. Its lock-up, or Cage, which stands on the small green known as St. Peter's Hill, is unusual in that it has a rounded roof of bricks. The steps at the side of the lock-up once led to a pump, enabling either buckets or carts to be filled. Francis Holcroft, one of the three non-conformist martyrs buried at Oakington, was once locked up here for preaching. The last inmate, in 1840, apparently showed his gratitude by setting fire to the straw bedding which had been provided for his comfort.

FIRE ENGINE HOUSE

Position: At Melbourn, 3 miles north-east of Royston.
Ordnance Map: 1:50,000 Cambridge, Newmarket and surrounding area.
Sheet No: Landranger 154.
Map Reference: 381448.

Access: Take the A10(T) from Royston to Melbourn. In centre of Melbourn turn left on to Station Road for Meldreth. The fire engine house is on the left-hand side of the road, diagonally opposite from All Saints Church.

Cambridgeshire has a number of drab looking little buildings, which used to house either hand- or horse-drawn 'engines', all of which appear to date from the early 19th century. Some have been converted to garages, others are unlettered and, thus, it is easy for the passer-by to be unaware of the building's past importance. However, Melbourn's is clearly signed and easy to find.

Fire was, and still is, a particular hazard in areas where thatched buildings are common. Before the days of a nationally-organised fire brigade, many insurance companies maintained their own horse-drawn fire engines. To prevent the wrong company being called out, many houses had on the wall a large metal plaque showing with which company the house was insured. These 'fire-marks' are now very rare.

SHEEN MILL

Position: At Melbourn, 3 miles north-east of Royston.
Ordnance Map: 1:50,000 Cambridge, Newmarket and surrounding area.
Sheet No: Landranger 154.
Map Reference: 380449.

Access: Take the A10(T) from Royston to Melbourn. In centre of Melbourn turn left on to Station Road for Meldreth. Sheen Mill, now a restaurant, is on the left-hand side of the road just past the Dolphin Lane junction, which is after the old Fire Engine House.

Because of the lowliness of the chalk hills, the streams of Cambridgeshire are slow-moving and meandering. Thus, prior to the Industrial Revolution, wind was a more reliable source of power than water. However, watermills were built and many have ground their corn and paid their tax since the Domesday Book, for example the mill at Houghton & Wyton. Most of these mills have since found a new lease of life as is the case with Melbourn's which is now a restaurant.

STOCKS & WHIPPING POST

Position: At Meldreth, 4 miles north-east of Royston.
Ordnance Map: 1:50,000 Cambridge, Newmarket and surrounding area.
Sheet No: Landranger 154.
Map Reference: 375465.

Access: Take the A10(T) from Royston to Melbourn. In centre of Melbourn turn left on to Station Road for Meldreth. The stocks and whipping post stand under a large chestnut tree on Marvell's Green at the junction of Fenny Lane and Manor Road.

The stocks and whipping post at Meldreth, the last in the county, are the village's 'landmark'. They are a reminder that justice was once a matter for the village or manor to deal with. The present whipping post was erected in 1782 at the cost to the parish of one shilling, and a new set of stocks replaced the former in 1833 at a cost of £3.2s. The last time the stocks were used was in the 1860s when one of the locals was placed in them for brawling in church. Beside the stocks can be seen the stone base of an ancient praying cross.

THRIPLOW SMITHY

Position: Village Green, Thriplow.
Ordnance Map: 1:50,000 Cambridge, Newmarket and surrounding area.
Sheet No: Landranger 154.
Map Reference: 436464.

Access: Take the A10(T) from Cambridge for Royston. At the entrance to Harston turn left on to the B1368 for Newton and Fowlmere. One mile after passing through Newton turn left on to the minor road for Thriplow.

The Old Smithy was presented to the village in 1964 by Robert J. Younger formerly of Thriplow Place. An inscription on a plaque on the Smithy bears the quotation:

By Hammer and Hand all Things do Stand.